Active Teaching  Learning Strategies

Creating  for Success

Rock D. Moore Ed.D
Michelle A. Moore M.Ed

Note for Librarians: a cataloguing record for this book that includes Dewey Decimal
Classification and US Library of Congress numbers is available from the Library and Archives
of Canada. The complete cataloguing record can be obtained from their online database at:
www.collectionscanada.ca/amicus/index-e.html
ISBN 1-4120-3660-7
Printed in Victoria, BC, Canada

TRAFFORD

Offices in Canada, USA, Ireland, UK and Spain
This book was published on-demand in cooperation with Trafford Publishing. On-demand
publishing is a unique process and service of making a book available for retail sale to the
public taking advantage of on-demand manufacturing and Internet marketing. On-demand
publishing includes promotions, retail sales, manufacturing, order fulfilment, accounting and
collecting royalties on behalf of the author.
Book sales for North America and international:
Trafford Publishing, 6E–2333 Government St.,
Victoria, BC v8t 4p4 CANADA
phone 250 383 6864 (toll-free 1 888 232 4444)
fax 250 383 6804; email to orders@trafford.com
Book sales in Europe:
Trafford Publishing (uk) Ltd., Enterprise House, Wistaston Road Business Centre,
Wistaston Road, Crewe, Cheshire cw2 7rp UNITED KINGDOM
phone 01270 251 396 (local rate 0845 230 9601)
facsimile 01270 254 983; orders.uk@trafford.com
Order online at:
www.trafford.com/robots/04-1488.html

10 9 8 7 6 5 4 3 2

TABLE OF CONTENTS

CHAPTER 3
Active Teaching Strategy II: Obtain and Maintain Student

CHAPTER 4

CHAPTER 5
Active Teaching Strategy IV: Immediate Feedback

CHAPTER 6
Active Learning: What Students Do

FORWARD

This book: **Active Teaching and Active Learning Strategies: Creating a Blueprint for Success**, is the cumulative result of a year of reflecting, asking, and listening to questions, and comments, that many have concerning the education of our youth. The book's genesis however, started many years ago as the state of California, along with many other states, embraced a standards based accountability system. This accountability has now been coupled with the recent addition of **The No Child Left Behind Legislation**. In a real sense, we are entering both the best and worst of times. I say this because of the effects of high-stakes testing and the requirement that all students reach high levels of proficiency which admittedly, are very lofty goals. For this to be realized, changes will be required in teaching and assessment, as well as a more concentrated focus on student learning.

The instructional design introduced in this book advocates four components: academic, social/collaborative, contextual, and cognitive/developmental. These components work in tandem with Active Teaching and Learning Strategies. Combined, they form a student responsive instructional methodology, which optimizes student success, and academic achievement.

We wanted to create a book that demonstrated to those of us in the field of education the value of looking at academic standards with data about our students, and reflecting on how this information should influence our choices concerning instructional practices and our perceptions about the students that we are entrusted with. The focus of this endeavor is to see all students achieve and succeed, and to keep passion and compassion at the heart of all that we do.

It is the premise of this book that the difference between effective and outstanding teachers are that outstanding teachers care, know how to utilize data, practice active teaching strategies, and promote the active learning of students. Together these characteristics became the design, and course of action, that **Created a Blueprint for Success.**

ACKNOWLEDGEMENTS

I would like to thank my husband for his ambitious passion and commitment to his wife, daughter, and profession. Rock is an amazing husband, phenomenal father, and consummate professional. Confident and successful in his balance, his drive has encouraged me in, what is now, our pursuit: to embrace the students of today, and continually strive to be *Active Teachers [with students who are] Active Learners: Creating a Blueprint for Success.*

He has been an inspiration to many, including myself. I consider it a privilege to be his wife and possess an insurmountable level of respect and adoration for his (our) quest in continually reaching, striving, and dedicating ourselves to the *blueprint in leaving no one behind.*

- Mrs. Michelle A. Moore

Any endeavor, done collectively, has its sweet rewards. I am thankful that I have a wife who shares the passion and understanding of what it is like to be in education today. As this book evolved, we bantered back and forth over philosophy, organization, theory, and practice, as it relates to teachers and administration. I am indebted to Michelle and the depth of her knowledge base, practical experience, and abundance of classroom applications. Without her continual feedback and outstanding editorial skills, we might still be on the first draft of this book.

- Dr. Rock D Moore

In addition, we would like to thank four other individuals. The first is our daughter Faith. Thank you for continually teaching us about being "human" and the importance of looking at each child as an individual. You teach both of us so much, and you do it without even knowing that you are. Secondly, a special thank you and an acknowledgement to Mrs. Adrian Ober. Your time, effort, energy, and expertise into editing the final edition of the book cannot be expressed enough. We are both indebted to you. Thank you for making this text a reality. Next, we would like to thank Mark Aiassa. He took our conceptual thoughts and translated them into the cover of this text. Finally, we would like to acknowledge Garret Briney whose pose graces the cover of this book. We thank all of you, again, for your contributions.

-The Authors

PREFACE

Collectively, my wife and I have over 25 years of experience in serving students. We have worked as K-8 teachers and administrators in both public and private schools. We believe that there is no greater or higher purpose than to see students achieve and succeed in school. This is a very tall order and one that demands a critical analysis of our practices. That very statement was and is the inspiration behind this book

The text original genesis was to address the academic, social, and behavioral needs of students who have been identified as at-risk. But, as we began to evaluate our specific schools and talk to other teachers and administrators, a decision was made to expand the parameters to include all students. This shift came about, in part because of the challenges of the No Child Left Behind legislation and the Adequate Yearly Progress requirements, which all schools are expected to reach.

In actuality, all educators face a myriad of personalities, issues, and challenges, when dealing with the diverse needs of a school community. We are expected to meet all of the needs of each group, despite the fact that in many cases, we have not been trained on how to implement new mandates ourselves. Unfortunately, this brings about a high level of frustration for both teachers and students. Worst yet, this frustration can impede the students' academic growth and a teacher's ability to be effective.

The objective of this book is to distill and bring together some of the most current research and practices to help all of our students succeed. It needs to be remembered that not all answers to educational issues are simple. The book will provide some "how-to-do" and "what-to-do's" to help answer questions that may be raised about personal practices, as well as issues generated by this publication.

This book's chapters and topics are arranged in a concise and easily accessible format. The topics can be located under the chapter headings in the table of contents.

HOW WE GOT HERE

Chapter One addresses some of the issues that all in education face. It is important to look at the landscape of where we are—it gives us the power to see what is, and then determine where we should be. Some negative perceptions about academic standards and student potentials are identified that inhibit student growth. Some of these voiced concerns include; *Parents of our students are illiterate, there is not enough time in a school day to address all students' needs, or the academic standards required are too difficult for our students.* Our question to the reader then is "now what?" If curricular changes are not implemented, then do we stay the same course and expect different results? Without this reflective process, we will never alter current practices. Other topics included in this chapter are:

- curriculum coverage,
- expectations,
- using and understanding demographic data, and
- learning styles.

FIRST ACTIVE TEACHING STRATEGY
CLEAR COMMUNICATION

Chapter Two opens the discussion on active teaching and student responsive instructional practices. It is about what teachers do. It is a design for success that provides an education for all children; taking into account the students learning styles and individual uniqueness. This design promotes a methodology that is proactive instead of reactive. These active strategies are then translated into outcomes that need to be communicated and reinforced to the students. In addition, concise steps are given that directly guide the students in their understanding, to successfully accomplish specific academic goals. The first active teaching strategy entails:

- academic content standards,
- directions that are clear, accurate, and precise,
- instructional guides that drives the curriculum, and
- the use and creation of performance based rubrics.

Rock and Michelle Moore MiRoc Publishing @ AOL.Com

SECOND ACTIVE TEACHING STRATEGY
OBTAIN AND MAINTAIN STUDENT ENGAGEMENT

Chapter Three describes practices to keep students actively involved. Most effective teachers vary their strategy use to promote student success. However, the distinctive difference between effective teachers who reach most students and outstanding teachers who reach all of them is the utilization of differentiated instruction that increases the students' time on task. Maintaining student engagement involves understanding what students understand. It is seeing assignments through their eyes and hearing instruction and information through their ears. This is important because much can be lost through the daily interactive process of the classroom. By continually engaging students, a teacher can discover potential barriers that can impede student learning as well as teaching them specific practices that will make them more productive. Highlights of this chapter include:

- varying the delivery methods,
- identify barriers to learning,
- utilize social and collaborative strategies,
- continually provide ample practice opportunities.

THIRD ACTIVE TEACHING STRATEGY
MONITORING STUDENT PROGRESS

Chapter Four discusses the importance of monitoring student success. Monitoring broadly defined is analyzing tasks performed against results. Monitoring necessitates regular reviewing, refining, and modifying the process to intensify the focus towards the desired results. Instructional strategies need to evolve from the analysis of student data and progress. Monitoring the student's strengths and challenges is vital in assessing their abilities to make sense of what they are learning and doing. Evaluation of student's strategies, what works, and why, are examined during the monitoring process. This allows the teacher to make procedural corrections, re-teach, clarify as needed, encourage students, as well as teach new strategies that will reduce time and promote student success. By continually monitoring the students, teachers can help choose which method, or combination of methods, are the most beneficial to accomplish a specific task. Progression charts, timelines, and anchor papers used in conjunction with clearly defined rubrics help demystify assignments and guide the students self-monitoring. Other topics in this chapter include:

- utilizing cognitive and developmental strategies,
- frequently monitoring and reviewing of student work,

- tailoring learning targets to individual needs (process data),

- adjusting instruction to maximize learning (formative/summative data),

- evaluation of strategy selection,

- creating prescriptive instructional practices.

FOURTH ACTIVE TEACHING STRATEGY
IMMEDIATE FEEDBACK

Chapter Five analyzes the importance of feedback and its impact on students. Short intervals for feedback have been found to be effective in evaluating the strategies used by students. In addition, this feedback guides the students to new and improved strategies for their individual success, as well as promoting ownership and motivation. Immediate feedback also increases self-efficacy, due in part to the students attributing the positive feedback to their own efforts and hard work. Learning activities can be organized in such a way that individual facts, processes, and principles are taught within the larger context of what is expected to be mastered at a certain grade level or within some established academic standard. Other topics on feedback include:

- promote contextual strategies,

- use of positive praise,

- student refinement, and

- continual academic refinement for student improvement.

ACTIVE LEARNING

Chapter Six demonstrates what students can do to learn how to become effective learners. Students will never do well if they do not try. Lack of effort can occur as a result of negative perceptions, attitudes, poor motivation, insufficient commitment, and lack of understanding. Therefore, students need to develop active learning strategies to understand and fulfill the academic requirements of any assignment. Without the skills associated with active learning, students will not have a repertoire of strategies to be able to make the necessary adjustments to complete assignments successfully. The end result of this cycle of failure is students, who are frustrated, and lack the confidence, or ability, within themselves to succeed.

Other topics highlighted in chapter six include:

- student perceptions,

- internalizing practices that promote success,

- independent learning, and
- characteristics of active learning.

CONCLUSION

We feel confident that this book will provoke questions that are germane to your classroom, school site, university classroom, or district. The strategies and instructional designs in this text are by no means exhaustive or all-inclusive. The volume is meant to be utilized as a basic reference tool or starter guide in using active teaching and learning strategies. Its intended users are teachers, professors, researchers, and administrators. We hope, if you have taken up this publication, you will find the information pertinent, the research solid, and the examples with standards usage relevant, current, and helpful, and that it will serve as a source for personal introspection and reflection to bring about a positive change in practice.

Rock and Michelle Moore MiRoc Publishing @ AOL.Com

INTRODUCTION

While the movement for state academic standards and performance assessments has succeeded in bringing about a greater awareness to the issues surrounding student achievement, very little attention has been given to what it takes to create conditions in the at-risk classroom that will make positive academic achievement a daily reality. By saying at-risk classrooms, the implications are that a significant portion of students in them have been identified as highly unlikely to succeed under current No Child Left Behind (NCLB) legislation, and its accompanying Adequate Yearly Progress (AYP) requirements.

The term at-risk, in this context, is not limited to traditional qualifiers or statistical indicators like; color, gender, socio-economic status, or where students live. Instead, the term is used in a broader context, encompassing students who are not meeting the new accountability requirements mandated by the federal government. For example, in California, on the latest standards-based assessments, about 10 percent of all students' scored in the advanced range, and another 25 percent scored in the proficient range. This translates to 65 percent of new students potentially being added to those labeled as at-risk (Manthey, 2004).

It is interesting to note, that absent from much of the political debate related to NCLB requirements and student success, is how to support and cultivate teaching practices, which inspire all students to heightened levels of academic achievement. According to Jamentz, there are growing numbers of educators and concerned parents who want answers to these questions. They want to know how many students are actually reaching the prescribed academic levels of proficient and advanced. In addition, they want to know the overall rate of academic success, and more importantly, what specific conditions in the classroom are the greatest contributors to positive student improvement (2001).

It must be acknowledged, at the onset of this book, that very little of the vast amount of educational research previously conducted appears to have had any noticeable impact on teachers or their classroom practice. This has occurred in part because of the unavailability of the research findings or conclusions. Much of the investigative work is conducted at the university level, and unless teachers are currently attending classes; investigating a specific topic, or are part of an actual study, they simply are unaware of the findings. Research conducted at the university level tends to stays there, or is printed in journals that the average educator at a school site does not subscribe to. In many cases, school personnel are not aware that these journals even exist.

Another problem is that a theory, or set of theories, may have been identified and defined at the university level, but have not been articulated in a way that is useful to the teacher or in a classroom context. Theoretical models must be made practical for students and teachers alike. Furthermore, many political mandates demand immediate student results. Therefore, without a blueprint that systematically shows how to promote student success, or at the very least, guides' educators in their understanding of how to reach the objectives, the mandates will never fully be realized.

Likewise, "until we get 100 percent of our students doing well, we are launched on a grand experiment, one that no nation has ever before made a part of its public policy" (Manthey, 2004, p. 23). It is our contention that a new and exciting era of educational practice and accountability has arrived. With this backdrop, schools and the educators in them are being challenged to become producers and analyzers of their own data, instead of consumers of others. Thus, many school sites are now actively identifying, analyzing, creating, and then implementing their own solutions. They are learning how to define their own remedies that are based on the students' academic needs in the context of their individual experiences. In this light, current and past practices are being revisited and analyzed to see what works, what does not, and the context in which one set of practices are more productive than others. The book was specifically designed and researched to explore these very topics. All ideas and concepts presented within this text have their roots of success in actual practice. Equally important, the methodology, principles, and their applications, are firmly based on highly regarded theories, which positively promote student success.

Rock and Michelle Moore MiRoc Publishing @ AOL.Com

CHAPTER 1

EDUCATIONAL THEORY AND PRACTICE

When educational theory is transformed into practice, principles employed by school administrators and teachers tend to be marginalized in relationship to classroom practice and instruction. This is due in part to time constraints, attitudes concerning students, and educational experience. In addition, there is a proclivity of late to reduce instructional plans to narrowly defined performance skills and academic standards that can be easily measured. The danger is that the overall needs of students are no longer at the core of the decision making process.

According to Sears and House (2002), the educational practices of schools serving low-income and minority students put their students at a greater incidence of risk simply because they employ the least qualified personnel. These individuals are the least qualified, not in terms of experience or educational level, but because of the philosophical constructs that they embrace. Their belief systems, whether it is on a conscious or subconscious level, are that their students do not have the ability to succeed.

Manthey (2004) takes this notion further. He quotes Jeff Howard as saying "…all of us categorize people into one of five groups: the really smart, the smart, the sorta smart, the kind-of dumb, and the really dumb (p. 23). Manthey then states that his guess is "…that lots of people think that the majority of children of poverty fit into the category of kind-of dumb" (p. 23).

In addition to possessing these negative convictions, some who work with at-risk students believe the requirements are just too high and unjust for those whom they have enrolled in their classrooms. They have concluded that the students' parents are uneducated, and do not care about their children's education. The criteria, set by states academic standards, are just unrealistic.

This mantra of negative beliefs are continually reinforced and perpetuated by school personnel. In turn, it is then internalized and embraced by the students, and evidenced in their attitudes about themselves. Thus, they see little connection between the skills taught in school and the hope for a better future. Data across many states, and the various school districts in them, indicate that poor students, and those of color, are systematically denied an education that leads them to success in school or in the workplace (Education Trust, 2000). Unfortunately, these numbers, because of the recent NCLB requirements, are increasing. This is occurring in part because the AYP does not measure growth in terms of student advancement from one year to the next. The new mandates only validate those students who reach the prescribed categories of proficient and advanced.

We are doing a very good job of educating 30 percent of our students. But the goal is to do a very good job with 100 percent. You may have come here [to the Gates Foundation for Principals in Kansas] hoping to find out how we are going to do that. No one knows, but if we keep our school system as it is we'll never reach that goal (Manthey, 2004, p. 23).

It needs to be noted that these least qualified individuals, those who embrace negative concepts about their students, are in a minority in the public school system. Still, they tend to get the majority of negative press. Although few in number, these educators are held up by some in the national media, as examples of what is wrong today with some public schools.

"Before we can rebuild our schools to places where 100 percent of our students do succeed, we need to rebuild our belief system. We must believe it can be done" (Manthey, 2004, p. 23). We, the authors' of this book, also embrace this concept. We believe that the principles of active teaching and learning will create a blueprint for success allowing all students to succeed.

LOW EXPECTATIONS

Conversely, there is a large body of research which clearly demonstrates that students in low expectation environments are the ones who ultimately suffer. This happens in part because their value as individuals has been depreciated. Instead of looking at all students as individuals and how best to help them succeed academically, socially, and behaviorally, they are minimized to statistical performance factors, such as:

- How well did the students perform on the states accountability test? or

- How high or low are their test achievement scores? or

- What interventions or remediation can be used to increase scores on their assessments?

In addition, the following protocols are commonly found in classrooms not adequately meeting the needs of students:

- The teacher knows what needs to be taught. If the students master the material they will be promoted. No connection needs to be made between the materials being taught or to the students themselves. Academic standards are meant to be mastered and that is one of the main goals of schooling.

- The students are passive and dependent on the teacher in part because the teacher possesses all that the student needs to know. The students never experience self-efficacy or develop a positive image because all learning, therefore all reinforcers, come from the teacher. Students perceive that what they know is not important, that they have very little to offer. In addition, direct instruction is the most effective and time honored strategy to communicate large amounts of information in a short period of time.

- The teacher is the manager of the class and therefore controls and uses one way discourse techniques to transmit knowledge and information to the student. A student's previous experience or knowledge is of little value in connecting to academic standards expected to be attained at each grade level.

- A teachers' job is to teach and the students' job is to learn. Cognitive, social, or developmental levels are not considered. Passing is dependent on mastery of grade level outcomes. Remediation or alternative drill measures, to get the students to learn by osmosis, are successful methods for students to master grade level standards.

- Teachers teach subject matter. Curriculum is organized according to a pattern best suited for the teacher. Contextualization is not an important concept for the students' understanding or classroom experience. Students' feelings and perceptions are not valued because knowledge, not classroom affect, is power. Classroom discussions, from an instructional viewpoint, tend to slow down the information and skills-delivery process.

- Grades motivate the students. Nothing is intrinsic; everything that motivates is external. Learning is a direct result of parental pressure or teacher approval/disapproval. Schooling is mandated by law not student choice.

Furthermore, the teaching plans and academic objectives at these schools do not take into account the unique needs and circumstances of their student population. "Teachers who view, as their sole responsibility, the dispersing of knowledge and information do well to rethink their teaching mission…" (Pajares, 2002, p. 120). Therefore, as students attempt to make sense of their schooling environment, they learn that the teacher either builds up their self-confidence through empowering strategies or dampens them—which ultimately puts them at-risk. Cooley, over one hundred years ago, talked about the notion of the "looking glass self" in which learners sense of self comes from their perceptions of how others see them (1902). Students are not mature enough to make accurate, self appraisals so they rely on others evaluation of them to form opinions about their self value, which in turn, influences their confidence and motivation. The earlier in school this occurs, the more devastating the consequences.

To illustrate this point further, when elephants are small they learn very quickly that the chain that controls them is stronger than they are. As they try to break free, the chain continues to restrain them. Eventually, they give up trying to free themselves. As the elephants mature and become stronger, the chain size remains the same. However, this is irrelevant, because the elephants, when they were younger, had given up trying to be free. Tragically, the correlation is that more often than not, students—like the elephants, let others define and bind them, and then never challenge those notions later in their school experience.

When students perceive that they are powerless, unappreciated, or cannot succeed, they have an increased tendency to become alienated and disillusioned with school and those employed in them (McCombs, 2003). The students' alienation is manifested through a high level of off-task classroom behaviors, procrastination, poor learning strategies, and various forms of cheating. The students' are basically putting in their time, being passive listeners, and contributing as little as possible to the classroom dynamics (Graham and Golan, 1991; Urdan, Midgley, and Anderman, 1998; Anderman, Griesinger, and Westerfield, 1998).

CHANGING DIRECTIONS, PERCEPTIONS, AND ATTITUDES

Therefore, to effectively counter these negative perceptions, requires the implementation of a student responsive pedagogy. These practices are a set of student responsive methods, which are congruent with the new NCLB requirements. The application of these techniques takes students from being considered at-risk, to those capable of reaching their at-promise potential. According to Lewis, this responsive pedagogy must be based on the following core beliefs:

- Children will achieve when they are effectively taught how to learn because achievement is not innately determined.

- All children come to school with a variety of individual strengths; our responsibility as educators is to discover and build upon these strengths.

- Schools that practice on how their practices affect students will be more productive than those that blame students, families, or poverty for underachievement.

- Each individual staff member must examine his or her beliefs and change practices [if necessary]...

- Schools should be considered excellent only when students of all racial and ethnic groups are achieving at high levels (Lewis, 2003, p. 260).

To convert these convictions into instructional practices requires a commitment to put everything on the line to improve the educational experience and achievement of all students (Thompson, 2003).

A system where all students are successful? It's going to take a lot more than what schools can do by themselves. But it will never happen until we rebuild our own minds and start seeing all children, at the very least, as kinda smart...When this is accomplished we'll tolerate nothing less than 100 percent of them being proficient and/or advanced (Manthey, 2004, p. 23).

This improvement begins with teachers who care and believe that their students can and will succeed. These teachers are competent in their subject matter, and are able to implement quality instructional strategies that the students can readily adapt. The confidence teachers have about their competence influences their ability to affect the students learning in a positive way that promotes self-efficacy and academic achievement (Ashton and Webb, 1986). This competence is coupled with the teachers' concerns about the students and their well-being. This active approach builds student-to-teacher trust, which stems from a core set of beliefs, that all students are important, can learn, and each will succeed. This confidence is continually reinforced by positive interactions that the students experience throughout the school day.

THE LEARNING PROCESS

According to Combs (1982), the learning process should always contain two aspects: exposure to new information and understanding of what that information means. However, a third aspect needs to be added; consideration of students' attitudes and perceptions about schooling and subject matter. Teachers know that they need to find ways to understand their students, create a context, and provide a safe environment before quality learning can take place (McCombs, 2003). If a teacher does not know the types of pressures that students are dealing with, academic and behavioral interventions will be ineffective and the learners shortchanged. Plans and strategies that do not address these concerns are diminished in their effectiveness to promote student success. Therefore, the learning process should minimally contain:

- Exposure to new information;
- understanding of what the information means; and
- consideration of students' perceptions about the subject matter.

It is a fact that all students are unique. Each have differences that include their emotional state, how quickly they learn, their preferred learning styles, their abilities, talents, maturity, as well as their personal perceptions about school, the teacher, and what they are learning (McCombs and Whisler, 1997). To address the needs of a student adequately, each needs to be viewed holistically. As such, their cognitive, physical, social, and emotional states must be considered. Without this approach to the wholeness of the student, optimal learning and achievement opportunities will be lost. This holistic construct, viewing the child as a whole person, is evidenced by the teachers' personal view of the curriculum and the pedagogical or instructional strategies employed.

PEDAGOGY AND CURRICULUM: AN INFLUENTIAL RELATIONSHIP

In general, pedagogy refers to the art or profession of teaching. In many ways pedagogy encompasses the individual philosophies of the teacher and permeates their concepts about how students think, learn, and what are the best teaching practices for the students.

Each of these teacher-held beliefs have a direct as well as an indirect impact on the classroom. In fact, the connection between pedagogy and curriculum is powerful for two distinct reasons.

- The first is that curriculum is a body of subject matter content that results in the attainment of specific targets, academic standards, or products.

- The second aspect of curriculum focuses on the learner, the process or affect of the classroom, and how students' needs are met.

DEMOGRAPHICS

With the second aspect of curriculum in mind, students' backgrounds and circumstances need to be evaluated and assessed in context to specific behavioral goals and academic outcomes that are critical in optimizing success. Easily obtained information that can be readily utilized for this purpose is demographic data. It is a reality that schools have no control over their demographical make-up. However, demographics contain valuable indicators that either help or hinder student growth. These include but are not limited to:

- Language fluency and proficiency,

- previous or preschool experiences,

- parental education levels, and

- location stability and mobility.

Collectively, these individual components play a vital role in understanding and helping students, as well as addressing their attitudes about schooling. Demographic data plays an essential role in discovering the uniqueness of all students and especially to those who are in at-risk circumstances. Conversely, demographic data used inappropriately is a pretext to justify low expectations and minimal academic achievement. Proper usage will always provide a catalyst for better understanding and higher student achievement. Whenever data makes victims out of students, a cycle of failure will result.

FIGURE 1.1 ANALYZING DEMOGRAPHIC FACTORS TO PROMOTE STUDENT SUCCESS

Some suggested ways to start using demographic data includes reflecting on the following questions.

- How does the physical make-up of your classroom effect the selection of specific teaching strategies?
- What are those strategies and which students are they targeted to help?
- Are the students' academic needs met with their current classroom placement?
- How do you know?
- Do you see specific growth?
- Are the students in the best educational setting? Would they benefit more from an alternative setting/teacher?
- Do you believe that all your students can succeed?
- Is the teacher appropriately credentialed to optimally address specific student needs? English language learning/Special Education/Correct subject area?
- Are the teaching, subject matter, and academic standards appropriate for grade level/needs of students?
- What specific insights can be gleaned from a students' family background to promote a targeted students' success?
- How are you using it?
- Are there any identifiable barriers that need to be specifically addressed to help students' succeed?
- What are they and how is it working?

Below is a list of additional factors that can be utilized to promote student success.

FIGURE 1.2 FACTORS THAT CAN BE USED TO ANALYZE SCHOOL-WIDE DEMOGRAPHICS

About Students
Number of students in school
Class size
Absence/tardies
Gender
Ethnicity/race
Home background
Lunch status (free, reduced, full price)
Language proficiency
Pre-school attendance

About Staff
Number of teachers, administrators,
Paraprofessionals and support staff
Years of experience (total number of years
and by grade level)
Absences
Gender
Ethnicity/race
Retirement projections
Types of certification
Student-teacher ratios
Professional development opportunities
Extracurricular activities
Community involvement
Special qualities/strengths
Turn over rate of teachers/staff
Community support
Programs offered

About the School
History
Safety/crime data
Special needs
Mobility/retention rates dropout rates
Graduation rates
Post-graduate employment/education
Extracurricular activities
Honors/advanced placement status
Employment during high school

About the Community
Location
History
Makeup of the population
Economic base
Population trends
Types of employers in the community
Projections of growth
Employment of parents
Community/business involvement
Support agencies
(Brenhart, 2003, p. 290)

Effective use of demographic data results in carefully planned strategies for both short and long term objectives. For student responsive instructional practices to be effective, short term planning needs to take center stage. Essential goals, sequential planning, enrichment activities, and possible obstacles for learning, need to be identified and addressed appropriately.

UNIQUE STUDENTS, UNIQUE CIRCUMSTANCES

It becomes readily apparent, when looking at demographic data, that no two learners come from the same backgrounds or have the same experiences. Each student is diverse, even when students come from the same social, cultural, or ethnic group (Sturtevant, 1998). In fact, over the last thirty years a significant amount of research has been conducted on what are the best teaching practices for teachers to use to facilitate learning. Much of this data has been used to try and define specific traits, particularly in relation to various ethnic and cultural groups or sub-groups. Unfortunately, much of this information has been overly generalized; in that, in any given group there are variations. Not all Native-Americans, or African-Americans, or any other group, will be motivated to acquire knowledge from a specific style of learning, or receptive to any one way of teaching. By stating this as a fact, is to grossly over simplify the data. Traits, trends, and a group's proclivity to a certain style may be identified, but any indicators beyond that are purely speculative. In reality, economics, social class, location, and language plays a more consequential role in influencing how a student learns in a specific context.

Thus, providing a quality education for all students is a challenge. Not only are the classrooms diverse, but so are the needs of the students. For example, when students seem to be struggling with the same academic task, their specific needs often differ. One student's problem with math may stem from the inability to read, while another struggles with the same math problem because of language, and a third does not know how to multiply. The goal then becomes one of finding realistic and efficient ways of instructing and helping all these students succeed.

LEARNING STYLES

Most teachers willingly provide a wide array of strategies to reach and address the students and their individual learning styles. But learning styles have little to do with what is learned; it has more to do with the academic conditions that promote and optimize learning. Learning styles have been described as a quality or an attribute within individuals that influences the way they learn. They describe:

- Individual variations in modes of perceiving, remembering, and thinking;

- distinguish ways individuals apprehend, store, transform, and utilize information;

- categorize learners in terms of educational conditions that they are most likely to learn; and

- predict amount of structure needed to facilitate student learning (Sullivan, 1997).

In a real sense, learning styles helps teachers in their methods and plans on how to best deliver material and information. Because there is no single teaching method which can reach every student, most teachers use a variety of methods and employ the ones they feel the most competent in using. The intent is to get the students to master specific goals or academic standards.

It must be remembered there is no magic "fix all" for student success. To assume there is a universally applicable way of learning and teaching, is to fall into the trap of a fixed, ridged, and finite world. In actuality,

We must fight against any single model, structure, method, or system of education. We must expand the freedom of schools to test new concepts …We must realize that, most often, life does not contain single truths but instead predicaments, competing views, and apparent conflicts. The public school system must value and allow multiple conceptions of education that students, parents, and faculty members can choose from—some purebreds, some hybrids, and some yet to be known, but all devoted to students…Ultimately, we must hold every school and district responsible for whether it has provided an education for all children (Glickman, 2001, p. 152).

Thus, teachers who are informed about their students provide a responsive curriculum that educates all and focuses on:

- Conceptual understanding, individual inquiry, and mastery of concepts [academic];
- use of social, collaborative, and group problem solving processes [social];
- contextual activities[contextualization], and a
- supportive and challenging environment [demographic and developmental] (Meece, 2003, Moore and Moore, 2004).

DATA DRIVEN METHODOLOGY

In addition, these teachers, as part of their methodology, must continually analyze data about their students. It needs to be noted that methodology should never be confused with methods. Methodology by definition implies a search for the truth. It is a set of reflective practices, done by teachers or administrators, which are meant to clarify, interpret, and help understand specific students' needs to better facilitate and optimize their academic success.

Briefly, the confusion between method and methodology has occurred in part because there is a tendency to use methodology as an adjective preempting it to mean orderly and systematic. This misuse obscures the conceptual distinction between tools of scientific investigation (methods) and the underlying principles, data, or theory (methodology) that determines the plan of how the tools will be used in actual practice. Thus, methodology in the classroom context refers to analyzing data about the students and their background; it gives the "why" behind the teachers' instructional choices. The more this is done, the more responsive the instruction will be. Putting a responsive instructional design into effective classroom practices entails four distinct instructional components. These are:

- academic,
- social/collaborative,
- contextual, and
- cognitive/developmental.

STUDENT RESPONSIVE INSTRUCTION

Together, these four instructional components address the needs and various learning styles of all students. The four components interact with each other in such a way that they promote student learning. It is a defined model, not to a ridged set of rules or formula, but fluid, in that it is responsive to students and their academic needs. This design has the greatest possibility of maximizing student success and assuring that all are provided with an appropriate and adequate educational experience (Moore and Moore, 2004).

FIGURE 1.3 FOUR COMPONENTS FOR A STUDENT RESPONSIVE INSTRUCTIONAL DESIGN

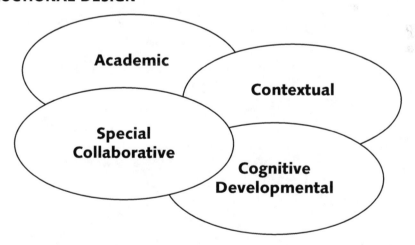

According to Glickman, there is no such thing as a single method, model, strategy, or plan that will work with every student, district, or situation. To claim this is to totally ignore any contradictions associated with these assertions.

The either/or debates about standards versus no standards...constructivist versus direct instruction...are symptomatic of ideologies that attempt to crush one another and leave only one solution standing...One group possesses the truth, and the other side is demonized as a pack of extremists...The real danger ...is the promotion of a single definition of a well educated citizen [instead of] public criteria based on data about student accomplishes and successes (Glickman, 2001, pp. 147-148).

The authors' purpose for mentioning this point is to acknowledge to the reader that no one piece of this model will stand alone on its own construct. It takes all four components working together to optimize student success. It also needs to be stressed that these practices are not derived from one philosophical belief system that is the common bond amongst the varied parts, but several that have been amalgamated together to make this instructional design. Many times educational theorist forget that in any classroom several theories are operating simultaneously and different theories work best with different applications.

CHAPTER 2

ACTIVE TEACHING STRATEGIES

In providing an education for all children, one that takes into account the students' learning styles and individual uniqueness requires an approach that is proactive instead of reactive. This proactive methodology is delivered best by the teacher to the students through the use of active teaching strategies. These strategies or outcomes need to be communicated and reinforced to the students. In addition, concise steps need to be utilized that directly guide students in their understanding. These practices help students successfully accomplish specific academic goals and tasks. Collectively, the four components directing teacher instructions are called active teaching strategies. They are: clear communication of academic tasks or requirements, obtaining and maintaining student's attention, monitoring of student progress, and providing immediate feedback.

ACTIVE TEACHING STRATEGY I: CLEAR COMMUNICATION

Teachers communicate clearly what students should know and be able to demonstrate by the end of a lesson or unit. This includes:

- Specifying what academic content standards are being addressed,
- giving clear and accurate directions, and
- indicating the type of rubric needed for students' self assessment.

To further develop the students' meta-cognitive development, and self-knowledge, the students' are active within the classroom. They discuss their understanding of the assignment with each other and explain why they are going to use a specific strategy or strategies to accomplish their specific goals.

ACADEMIC CONTENT STANDARDS

Over the past decade, many states have embraced academic performance standards which have helped define and demystify the academic criteria that students are expected to reach. The purposes of the standards are to define clear expectations of what students should master at each grade level. It is a criterion set that all students are expected to reach. Each standard has content that needs to be learned by students as well as some form of performance measurement that assesses students' progress towards attainment of those core content objectives. When implemented properly, the academic standards have the capacity to guide both teachers and students in a positive direction. The standards are a viable tool giving one the essentials needed for the students to achieve academic success. Teachers and staff embrace the notion that all students can learn and meet these high academic and performance standards. Ample evidence suggest that students learn best when the classroom instructional focus is on mastery of academic goals (Ames, 1992; Stipek, 2002). While acknowledging that some students must overcome significant barriers, these obstacles are not seen as insurmountable (Shannon, 2003).

Specifically, the standards:

- Focus on specific subject matter that needs to be delivered to each student at each grade level, and

- should expose, elaborate, bring about mastery, increase application, or become some form of generalized information available for the students' use.

The academic standards establish a minimum baseline for all students that are:

- Fair, impartial and just,

- equitable, unbiased, intended for everyone, and

- attainable, realistic and reachable.

The academic standards increase teacher productivity because they are a starter list of sorts to:

- Monitor peripheral issues that are not considered essential to student success or grade level expectancies.

- Focus direction and type of assessment that is performance based, accurate, relevant, and directly related to the academic standards taught.

- They give new teachers a framework to help in understanding grade specific competencies that their students are expected to know.

The academic standards increase student time on task because:

- Instruction is maximized with required content that all students are expected to master.

- Various standards can be interwoven together to help facilitate academic achievement.

- Following the standards reduce transition time between various levels of subject matter because teachers know where they are going (Moore, 1999a).

To illustrate, two California Language Arts Standards have been isolated to demonstrate what students are expected to master in regards to Reading Comprehension (2.0) and Literary Response and Analysis (3.0). Within each academic standard are sub-skills that guide both the teacher and student to achieve optimal success. It needs to be noted that the California Academic Standards have been used throughout this document as an example or reference point. However, any state or national standards can be substituted to best meet specific requirements or mandates.

STANDARD 2.0 READING COMPREHENSION STATES:

Students read and understand grade-level appropriate material. They draw upon a variety of comprehension strategies as needed (e.g., generating and responding to essential questions, making predictions, comparing information from several sources). In addition to their regular school reading, students read one half million words annually, including a good representation of grade-level-appropriate narrative and expository text (e.g., classic and contemporary literature, magazines, newspapers, online information).

Structural Features of Informational Materials

1.1 Identify structural patterns found in informational text (e.g., compare and contrast, cause and effect, sequential or chronological order, proposition and support) to strengthen comprehension.

Comprehension and Analysis of Grade-Level-Appropriate Text

2.2 Use appropriate strategies when reading for different purposes (e.g., full comprehension, location of information, personal enjoyment).

2.3 Make and confirm predictions about text by using prior knowledge and ideas presented in the text itself, including illustrations, titles, topic sentences, important words, and foreshadowing clues.

2.4 Evaluate new information and hypotheses by testing them against known information and ideas.

2.5 Compare and contrast information on the same topic after reading several passages or articles.

2.6 Distinguish between cause and effect and between fact and opinion in expository text.

2.7 Follow multiple-step instructions in a basic technical manual (e.g., how to use computer commands or video games).

3.0 LITERARY RESPONSE AND ANALYSIS STATES:

Students read and respond to a wide variety of significant works of children's literature. They distinguish between the structural features of the text and the literary terms or elements (e.g., theme, plot, setting, characters).

Structural Features of Literature

3.1 Describe the structural differences of various imaginative forms of literature, including fantasies, fables, myths, legends, and fairy tales.

Narrative Analysis of Grade-Level Appropriate Text

3.2 Identify the main events of the plot, their causes, and the influence of each event on future actions.

3.3 Use knowledge of the situation and setting and of a character's traits and motivations to determine the causes for that character's actions.

3.4 Compare and contrast tales from different cultures by tracing the exploits of one character type and develop theories to account for similar tales in diverse cultures (e.g., trickster tales).

3.5 Define figurative language (e.g., simile, metaphor, hyperbole, personification) and identify its use in literary works (English Language Arts Framework for California Public Schools, 1998, pp. 114-115).

It is important to remember that the minimum requirements for students at any grade level are the mastery of the academic standards. Therefore, before a teacher starts to instruct; in any curricular subject, do any project, unit, or activity, the first four questions that must be addressed are:

- What are the academic goals?
- Have I clearly communicated what is required?
- Are my plans helping students reach their objectives?
- Do the students know the assessment criteria?

These questions are specific to each classroom and there will be a wide variance in application depending on the subject matter and students being taught. However, the minimum requirements should be mastery of the content. If the lesson objectives do not meet or exceed academic standards, stop and reevaluate. Too often classroom activities are created that the students like, they are fun and the teacher enjoys doing them. Even so, they do not promote academic objectives as measured by performance-based or state mandated test. In reality, creativity should always be encouraged, but never at the point of failing to reach an academic objective.

CAUTIONARY CONCERNS

Likewise, it needs to be briefly mentioned that academic standards are not the same as student expectations. Student expectations are connected to previous achievement and perceptions held by both the student and teacher. Academic standards, on the other hand, are mandated by the state and the performance levels are set for all students. Similarly, academic standards and standards-based materials do not necessarily attain the same objective; namely mastery of specific academic standards.

> When teachers use standards aligned curriculum materials as the sole means of meeting standards, they are not given the opportunity to consider deeply the high expectations that the state frameworks describes for their students…Experience shows that teaching with standards aligned materials isn't enough to ensure that students meet [academic] expectations (O'Shea, 2003, pp. 22-23).

The most commonly observed errors when relying only on standards-aligned texts include: (a) too many academic standards selected for one lesson; (b) standards not correlated with curricular materials used; (c) standards selected were not at the appropriate grade level; (d) standards selected did not match the concepts of the lesson, (e) student activities and work products did not match performance outcomes related to the academic standards. In addition,

> Our California frameworks include teaching ideas, suggestions for finding instructional resources, vignettes of teaching episodes and teaching tips for teachers. While these ideas are helpful, it is the student learning expectations found in various locations within the frameworks that demand close inspection by teachers. These are the statements that explicitly describe what students are to know or be able to do to meet the standards. The selected standard and indicator and the descriptive statements pertaining to the selected indicator are the critical state-provided inputs to the standards-based lesson. From these inputs, decisions about curriculum are made - not visa versa (O'Shea, 2003, p. 23).

GIVING CLEAR AND ACCURATE DIRECTIONS

By creating standards-driven lessons, and tasks that have been created after careful thought, reflection, and the use of clear and accurate directions, appropriate corrective measures can be effectively implemented. Below is a sample lesson plan for social science/history. It has been designed to list the academic standard as well as a scoring rubric. Rubrics are generally defined as predetermined objective criteria, which have been established for assessing performance expectations on a particular topic. The more a teacher is explicit about their evaluation and assessment procedures, the greater the likelihood that the students will understand, embrace, and develop, the skills needed to achieve academic excellence. Included in this example are some suggested instructional strategies, meaningful learning activities, along with other written, oral and visual assessment task.

Before starting a lesson, a teacher can assess students' prior knowledge by determining:

- What the students already know about the specific topic or subject

- (similar to the utilization of the "K" in a K,W, L chart);

KNOW	WANT TO KNOW	LEARN

- draw a web to related terms, themes, or vocabulary; and

- make sure students know when assignment is due so that they can plan accordingly.

In this manner, a teacher can assess the students' understanding of the requirements on a particular subject or theme. It also allows both the teacher and students time to correct any misinformation or reinforce and re-teach material missed during initial instruction. This strategy is an effective way to activate prior knowledge or stimulate and prepare students for new insights. It is a useful technique for the teacher to use to view the "classroom landscape." This practice helps determine what the students really know about a given subject, topic, or standard.

FIGURE 2.1 DESIGNING A STANDARDS-BASED HISTORY/SOCIAL SCIENCE INSTRUCTIONAL PLAN

An outstanding instructional plan needs to contain several elements to be effective for the students. Specific academic standards, time frame, type of task, and their accompanying assessments and grading criteria, need to be established and clearly communicated. What follows are some suggested ideas that can be used to design a lesson. Its format is only meant to "prime the reader's creativity" and not serve as the accepted or only framework to create a lesson.

Grade Level   Time Frame (Give timeline to students)
Lesson Title:
Example History/Social Science Academic Content Standard(s) for the 5th Grade:

5.11 Describe how geography and climate influence the way various nations lived and adjusted to the natural environment, including location of villages, the distinct structures that they build, and how they obtain food, clothing, tools, and utensils.

5.2 Have students trace the route of early explorers and describe the early explorations of the Americas.

The Academic Content Standards: Listed below are some additional across the curriculum examples that cover several different grade levels and standards. These academic standards could be taught, reinforced, or implemented through the history/ social science instructional time to further enhance the lesson. This is only an example and it is not suggested that different grade level standards be mixed within a lesson. The standards are only meant to provide a stimulus to the reader.

Language Arts Writing Standard for the 5ᵗʰ Grade:

2.3 Write a research paper about important ideas, issues, or events by using the following guidelines: (a) frame questions that direct the investigation; (b) establish a controlling idea or topic, (c) develop the topic with simple facts, details, examples, and explanations.

Visual and Performing Arts Content Standards for the 5ᵗʰ Grade:

5.3 Research and report on various types of artists (e.g., architects, designers, graphic artist, animators), explain how their work plays a role in our everyday life.

English Language Development Standards for the 5ᵗʰ Grade:

Collect information and take notes on a given topic from a variety of sources (e.g., dictionary, library books, research materials).

Historical and social sciences analysis skills: What are the student learning outcomes in each area listed below:

- Chronological and Spatial Thinking:

- Research, Evidence and Point of View:

- Historical Interpretation:

- Other Academic Content Standard(s):

- **Designing Instruction:** What instructional strategies will be provided to enable all students to successfully participate in the learning opportunities listed below. Strategies vary depending on outcome objectives and the needs of each student. It is important to identify possible barriers to learning and list strategies to counter these obstacles.

- **Motivational Strategies:** How will the lesson be started? What is going to grab the students' attention; especially those whom are the least interested.
  Examples:
  1. Realia
  2. Pictures
  3. Historical book/picture/document/film clip
  4. Role play
  5. Character in costume
  6. Multi-media presentation

- **Accommodations:** What support systems or balance of instructional strategies will be provided so that each student has an opportunity to learn in the most effective way for them?
  Examples:
  1. Targeted vocabulary
  2. Glossary of terms
  3. Visuals
  4. Classroom notes/partials
  5. Integrated vocabulary

- **Learning Opportunities:** What will students need to do to achieve the knowledge and skills identified in the standard(s) and learning outcomes? Describe the instructional activity or activities that will engage students. Learning opportunities should be culturally sensitive and address multiple learning styles of students.
  Examples:
  1. Analyze a historical document, video, or documentary
  2. Play knowledge bingo
  3. Visit a museum
  4. Do a research paper/project/poster
  5. Examine and analyze visuals i.e., political cartoons, pictures, realia, charts, maps
  6. Role play a historical or political character
  7. Reenact a famous scene
  8. Create/make a learning game/activity
  9. Watch/critique a performance
  10. Participate in a debate
  11. Create a historical newspaper/headline
  12. Write a poem about a specific historical event

FIGURE 2.2 EXAMPLE ASSESSMENT TASK

What specific student product(s) and/or performance(s) will provide evidence of student learning? This is an essential component because it serves as a precursor to set up the rubric.

Written	Oral	Visual
Autobiography	Commercials	Banner
Biography	Debate	Cartoon
Biographical sketch	Dialogues	Chart/T-chart
Book report/review	Dictate sentences	Collage
Character portrait	Simple stories/story	Collection
Crossword puzzle	Endings	Computer graphic
Description	Discussion	Construction
Dialogue/script	Dramatization	Data table
Editorial	First person narrative	Design
Essay	Interview	Diagram
Diary	Newscast	Display
Game	Oral presentation	Diorama
Instructions	Oral report	Drawing
Invitations	Play	Filmstrip
Journal	Poetry reading	Graph
Labels and captions	Rap	Graphic organizer
Letter-business	Role play	Grid/matrices
Personal letter-to the editor	Skit	KWL chart
Log	Song	Map
Magazine article	Speech	Model
Memo	Teach a lesson	Outline
Notetaking/notemaking		Painting
Newspaper article		Photograph
Persuasive writing		Poster
Poem		Scrapbook
Postcard		Sculpture
Proposal		Slide show
Questionnaire/survey		Storybook
Reader's Theater		Tableau
Research report		Timeline
Rules		Venn diagram
Resume		Webbing/mind mapping

The above assessment task helps students focus on specifically defined targeted goals, standards, or objectives, which need to be mastered or accomplished.

Assessment/Rubrics-Public, Posted, Predetermined (A rubric is a matrix of sorts. It is utilized to reinforce clear and accurate assessment expectations and to measure attainment levels of the assessment task). Rubrics determine what students will need to do to demonstrate achievement of the standard(s) and learning outcomes. The assessment task should provide students with various options for demonstrating achievement.

FIGURE 2.3 SUGGESTED CHARACTERISTICS OF A RUBRIC: ARTICULATED CRITERIA FOR SUCCESS AND STUDENT SELF-ASSESSMENT

- A rubric helps students self-evaluate as well as define the outcomes expected. In addition, rubrics contain the characteristics that need to be met to receive a specific grade or score.

- Assessment criteria are a central feature of standards based assignments.

This is a philosophical shift from what the teacher is teaching to measuring what the students are learning.

- Rubrics assist in the process of teaching more efficiently because there is a

direct link between instruction and assessment.

- A public rubric is a meaningful way of promoting students' self-efficacy and self-confidence because it is a map of sorts for them to monitor their task.

EXAMPLE STANDARDS FOR RUBRIC DEVELOPMENT

Language Arts-Writing 3rd Grade

1.4 Revise drafts to improve the coherence and logical progression of ideas by using an established rubric. i.e., six trait writing, etc.

Visual and Performing Arts-Theatre 7th Grade

4.1 Develop and apply appropriate criteria or rubrics for critiquing…

Science-Investigation and Experimentation 5th Grade

6a Classify objects (e.g., rocks, plants, leaves) in accordance with appropriate criteria.

FIGURE 2.4 FRAMEWORK FOR RUBRIC CONSTRUCTION

The matrix below demonstrates one way to design a rubric with the corresponding standards and scoring criteria.

Point Value or Grade	1st Elements of Criteria Needed	2nd Elements of Criteria Needed	3rd Elements of Criteria Needed	4th Element of Criteria Needed
Point Value A or 4	Descriptors of Highest level of Completion	Descriptors of Highest level of Completion	Descriptors of Highest level of Completion	Descriptors of Highest level of Completion
Point Value B or 3	Descriptors of Mastery level of Completion	Descriptors of Mastery level of Completion	Descriptors of Mastery level of Completion	Descriptors of Mastery level of Completion
Point Value C or 2	Descriptors of Basic level of Completion	Descriptors of Basic level of Completion	Descriptors of Basic level of Completion	Descriptors of Basic level of Completion
Point Value D or 2	Descriptors of Lowest level of Completion	Descriptors of Lowest level of Completion	Descriptors of Lowest level of Completion	Descriptors of Lowest level of Completion

SAMPLE RUBRICS

Below are three examples of rubrics with each serving a different purpose. However, each has the common elements of descriptors and point values for the assessment of quality. These examples are meant to serve as a starter list and do not constitute the "correct" or only way to develop a rubric. Its purpose is to serve as a catalyst for the readers to develop their own objective criteria when designing specific tasks.

FIGURE 2.5 ROCKET RACER REPORT: SCIENCE RUBRIC

Science-Investigation and Experimentation 7th grade

7e Communicate the steps and results from an investigation in written reports and oral presentations.

The checklist/rubric needs to include the following:

_____ Research notes attached from all team members.

_____ Presentation levels need to addressed.

_____ Team member's ability to answer questions confidently.

_____ Team members list and use vocabulary from the unit accurately.

_____ Presentation demonstrates creativity and holds interest of class.

_____ All team members participated.

Rocketry	PowerPoint Research	Labs Worksheets	Presentation	Rocket Building
EXPLOSIVE 4	8 slides Title on each slide Picture on each slide Animation on each slide Facts relevant to topic	Completed 4 labs Completed charts/graphs All sketches drawn All answers in complete sentences	Turned in research notes when due Appropriate voice level Answered questions with confidence	Design turned in on time Altitude of 30 + meters Journal and Reflections Creative
FIERY 3	6-7 slides Title on each slide Picture on 5-6 slides Animation on 5-6 slides Facts relevant to topic	Completed 4 labs Incomplete charts/graphs All sketches drawn Not all answers in complete sentences	Turned in research notes day late Voice level not loud enough Answered most questions	Design turned in on time Altitude of 30 + meters Journal and Reflections Creative
FIZZLE 2	5-6 slides Title on 5-6 slides Picture on 3-4 slides Animation on 3-4 slides Facts relevant to topic	Completed 3 labs Incomplete charts/graphs Poor sketches Answers in one word sentences	Turned in research notes 2 days late Voice level low Answered few questions	Design turned in on time Altitude of 30 + meters Journal and Reflections Creative
DUD 1	4 or less slides Fewer than 3 titles Picture on 2 or less No animation Facts not relevant	Completed less than 3 labs Incomplete charts/graphs No sketches No answers to questions	Did not turn in research notes Voice barely audible No questions answered	Design turned in on time Altitude of 30 + meters Journal and Reflections Creative

Created by Sandra Briney and Cindy Bjelland, Summer 2003.

Rock and Michelle Moore MiRoc Publishing @ AOL.Com

FIGURE 2.6 RUBRIC FOR ORAL PRESENTATION

EXAMPLE STANDARDS FOR ORAL PRESENTATION

Listening and Speaking 10th Grade.

1.12 Evaluate the clarity, quality, effectiveness, and general coherence of a speaker's important points, arguments, evidence, organization of ideas, delivery, diction, and syntax.

English Language Development.

Analyze how clarity is affected by patterns of organization, hierarchical structures, repetition of key ideas, syntax, and word choice in text across context areas.

Score 5 - Excellent

Enthusiastic about Presenting/Talking. Uses excellent expression. Speaks well in phases or groups of words. Does not lose place while presenting. Speaks at an appropriate rate of speed. Comprehends what has been stated. Answers questions from audience clearly.

Score 4 - Very Good

Appears to enjoy presenting/talking. Uses good expression. Speaks fairly well in phrases or groups of words. Does not lose place while presenting. Speaks at appropriate rate of speed. Comprehends what has been read. Answers questions from the audience clearly.

Score 3 - Good

Presents to fulfill the assignment. Speaks at slow rate or speed. Speaks in phrases or groups of words. Comprehends what has been read. Questions from the audience are answered partially.

Score 2 - Limited

Does not like to speak. Speaks with little expression. Speaks in short phrases or groups of words or may speak in a word-by-word manner. Does not fully comprehend what is read. Questions from the audience are answered with minimum effort.

Score 1 - Poor

Speaks because of assignment. Speaks with no expression. Speaks word-by-word or at a very slow rate of speed. Does not comprehend what is read. Questions from the audience receive only the most basic or no response at all.

Score 0 - Failed

Makes no attempt to present/talk.

FIGURE 2.7 GENERIC ASSIGNMENT RUBRIC

History and Social Science Analysis Skills 9th-12 Grades

4 Students construct and test hypothesis; collect, evaluate, and employ information from multiple primary and secondary sources; and apply it in oral and written presentations.

Visual and Performing Arts-Visual Arts 8th Grade

4.4 Develop and apply a set of criteria as individuals or in a group to assess and critique work...

Outstanding

Assignment fully accomplishes this criterion in an outstanding manner. Assignment was clearly focused on this criterion and has been exemplary in reflecting this focus through the presentation. Assignment demonstrates extensive effort to analyze and express this criterion through the research and presentation. This criterion could not be improved upon.

Excellent

Complete criterion in a thorough manner. Assignment was focused on the criterion and has clearly reflected this focus in the presentation. Assignment demonstrates effort to analyze and express this criterion through research and presentation. Assignment is well above-average on this criterion.

Good

Substantially completes the criterion, with some ideas or concepts missing. Assignment has made an attempt to analyze this criterion and has indicated this effort through the research and/or the presentation. Assignment is above-average on this criterion.

Satisfactory

Partially completes the criterion, with superficial analysis. Although assignment was not clearly focused on this criterion, some effort was made to address the criterion in either research or presentation.

Minimal

Minimally completes the criterion with inconsistent results. Assignment was not focused on this criterion and shows little effort in dealing with the criterion in either research or presentation.

Needs Work

Shows little evidence of having attempted to accomplish this criterion. Assignment does not appear to have focused on the criterion and does not demonstrate student understanding of the criterion through either research or presentation.

FIGURE 2.8 EVALUATIVE ESSAY

In summing up the rubric and assessment practices needed for the first active teaching strategy, a final suggestion to measure what students have learned is to write a brief essay. This can be conducted at the end of a class, period, topic, or theme. The purpose of the essay must be clear.

- Is the essays purpose to show understanding of knowledge gained, specific points of interest, convincing aspects, etc?

- Is it to demonstrate directions that were not clear or confusing?

- Is it about class time or homework assignment relating to lesson?

- How long will students be given to write essay (i.e., ten minutes at the end/ start of class, homework, one hour, etc.)?

- With above constraints, what is expected length of paper?

Obviously, not all learning activities are meaningful for every student. This type of formative activity allows immediate feedback to determine the rate that students understood the lesson directions and academic objectives. It clearly is a tool to assess the level of student mastery of material relative to what had been taught. This further helps the teacher in relationship to creating future assignments and making appropriate adjustments. Finally, the essay format can be used to analyze a rubrics effectiveness on focusing task that define and direct students to a successful completion on a given topic.

CHAPTER 3

ACTIVE TEACHING STRATEGY II: OBTAIN AND MAINTAIN STUDENT ENGAGEMENT

The second active teaching strategy is used to obtain and maintain student engagement. The purpose is to keep students actively involved. Active involvement helps students concentrate on specific practices that are productive, and helps them accomplish and master specific academic standards. This can be achieved by:

- **Varying the delivery methods;**
- **identifying barriers to learning;**
- **utilize social and collaborative groupings; and**
- **continually provide ample practice opportunities.**

VARYING DELIVERY METHODS

Effective teachers vary their strategy use to promote student success. This is important because most teachers have been adequately trained to find effective ways to reach most of their students. However, the distinctive difference between effective teachers who reach most students and outstanding teachers who reach all of them is the masterful use of differentiated instruction. This differentiation optimizes student participation by keeping them actively involved.

Likewise, maintaining student engagement involves understanding what students understand. It is seeing assignments through their eyes and hearing instruction and information through their ears. This is important because much can be lost through the dynamic process of giving and receiving of instruction. By continually engaging students, a teacher can discover potential barriers that can impede student learning, as well as make immediate corrections to further facilitate learning.

The older students are, the more information they have been exposed to. Some students learn material in a specific context and understand it others do not. This creates a dilemma for the teacher because some of the student's background information is incomplete, inaccurate, and therefore, hinders new learning. These barriers not only hamper their understanding, but also the students' attitudes, values, and perceptions. When these barriers exist, it becomes difficult for a teacher to keep the students focused.

IDENTIFYING BARRIERS TO LEARNING

One effective practice to counter these obstacles involves starting a classroom topic or discussion by asking students what they think is a fair answer to a specific question. Example, Was it appropriate for Goldilocks to enter the house of the three bears? What were the most important issues that the Pilgrims faced when they arrived at Plymouth? Did the individuals (Native Americans, Indians) who already lived there want the same "freedoms" that the Pilgrims wanted?

- Students can respond orally or the class can write responses on a piece of paper.

- This format can be adapted to a questionnaire that the students use to circle their answers.

- The process can be individualized or used as a group activity in which each group comes up with their response and explains why they chose a particular line of thinking.

- It can be used anonymously or with individual or group names. And finally,

- Are the students' assessments of the topic true, not true, or are they just not sure? This is a quick format to identify and remedy any misconception that the students may have embraced. If this technique is too difficult of a task because of the age of the students or the controversial nature of the topic, another strategy that can be used in the same way is the:
  - who,
  - what,
  - where,
  - when,
  - why, and
  - how format.

This technique allows students to separate information into smaller parts and then analyze each part. Students' interest is maintained because they can rapidly assess what information they have mastered, and what material needs to be looked at more closely. For some students, the smaller chunking or segmentation of information is more manageable, keeps them focused, and builds motivation.

When this strategy is first used, modeling helps the students internalize the practices and make it their own. This not only maintains student engagement and develops critical thinking; it is useful in developing their personal active learning strategies. Likewise, this practice helps the teacher understand what the students are not comprehending, or where they have become confused in the delivery of the material. It is a clear reference point on discovering barriers, and evaluating if the strategies being utilized by the teacher are effective, for the specific students, and their specific needs.

UTILIZING SOCIAL AND COLLABORATIVE STRATEGIES

We must remind ourselves that learning is one of the most fascinating and rewarding activities for human beings. The desire to learn, to discover, to figure something out, and to be able to do something well enough to proclaim it as one's own must surely be strong as any impulse in the human soul. Children cannot not learn. If they lose their appetite for school learning, it is because some person or some system has turned a natural, joyous activity into a form of drudgery, a theater of the absurd, or worse, a chamber of abuse (Fried, 2001, p. 127).

Active teaching builds on the desire to learn and discover by keeping the students actively engaged. It is an instructional truth that comprehension is increased when students experience a supportive learning environment and have opportunities to interact with each other. Dewey (1916) states that, "Education is not an affair of telling and being told, but an active and constructive process. Why is it, in spite of the fact that teaching by poring in, learning by a passive absorption, are universally condemned but so entrenched in practice?" (p. 46). Students need to have an active role in the process of acquiring knowledge and mastering the academic content. In classrooms where teachers employed social instructional practices, research shows that students placed a higher value on learning, and stayed on task when engaging in other meaningful classroom activities (Ryan and Stiller, 1991; Valeski and Stipek, 2001). Furthermore, the students become expressive because the interactive aspect of the class provides a high level of support. This support from both the teacher and peers helps to motivate the students to take risks. Likewise, assignments can be linked directly to specific academic standards so the students have many opportunities to gain mastery as well as receive meaningful feedback from peers.

Piaget (1976), states that students acquire knowledge through interactive and socially constructive processes. Their level of understanding and enhancement is directly related to their prior experiences that are triggered during the time of student to student, and student to teacher interactions. Students come to know a new concept by applying knowledge of previous learned ideas to the new information they are learning. Understanding is based on the reconstruction of meaning. Such reconstruction is established from the amalgamation of previous experience, familiarity with concepts, and a general understanding of the language and vocabulary used. The importance of this interactive ambiance can not be overlooked.

DIAGNOSTIC BACKGROUND ASSESSMENT

Students' previously learned information can be easily assessed by the teacher. Two simple ways to ascertain what information the students already know is through the method of asking key questions and the practice of starting with the end result in mind.

- The first, asking key questions, centers on analyzing responses to a student's prior knowledge base.

1. When was the Revolutionary War fought?

2. What nations were involved?

3. Name a general who later became a president?

This activity can be done either individually or in a group setting by using a questionnaire, multiple choice questions, or using a chalkboard or overhead and conducting an open forum in the classroom.

- The second approach, starting with the end in mind, is used to measure previously acquired knowledge to new information that needs to be mastered.

1. What do students need to learn to master these specific standards?

2. How many of the students are currently familiar with some of the information?

3. What are their various levels of understanding and depth?

4. Why is it important that the students learn this information? What is the overall purpose?

Assessing background information is much more than determining a student's readiness to learn or levels of mastery of certain principles and skills. It is about their ability to understand and amalgamate new ideas. Validation and application of prior knowledge influences the students to trust in their own problem solving skills and encouraging them to try applying these skills to other challenging situations.

By ascertaining the amount of prior knowledge a student possesses, a teacher can make decisions about instructional strategy use, revisions concerning classroom materials, starting points for a lesson, and indicators to create assessment rubrics to guide the students to a successful outcome. Thus, the teacher knows potential academic and behavioral problem areas and works with the students, knowing that advanced thinking skills are developed in a positively charged environment (Cotton, 2000).

IMPORTANCE OF INTERACTION

The dynamics of interaction between peers and the teacher, along with the student's ability to experiment and use several learning strategies, forms the basis for a deeper comprehension of what is being taught and learned. Discussions are not limited to clarifying each others questions or responses, instead:

- it is about giving truthful; and

- accurate information; with

- positive and meaningful feedback.

The instructional practices are continually adapted and modified to enhance learning. In addition, discussions serve as a genesis for future topics and themes within the specific academic genre.

Interactive practices helps form a personalized environment in the classroom and increases the chances for a positive learning experience for all students. The students perceive a sense of belonging, due in part to receiving help, recommendations, and advice that are consistent with their varied levels of maturity. If a specific strategy is not working to a students' advantage, they have the ability to pull from a wide array of alternative strategies. These strategies, suggested by both peers, and the teacher, can then be utilized to complete the task at hand.

This responsive interaction provides numerous advantages for all involved. When students learn in groups, the cognitive functions and multiple roles required to carry out various tasks can be displayed by different individuals and modeled for others to learn. Another asset is the students' ability to challenge misconceptions and misunderstandings about a lesson with their peers. Lastly, a group's synergy occurs increasing the use of new or improved problem solving strategies. Collectively, this results in the creation of positive classroom norms where effort and problem solving are valued and encouraged.

Furthermore, Dewey (1916) argued that children who engaged in task-oriented dialogue with peers reached a higher level of understanding than that attained by students who passively listened to a teacher's presentation. Piaget and Inhelder (1969) found that peers serve well in facilitating cognitive development amongst each other when they engaged in problem solving for academic purposes. Interactive dialogue between both the teacher and students, as well as between students themselves, in small groups, has shown a positive correlation towards increased oral language skills as well as a deeper level of comprehension. In fact, as students mature and grow older, they tend to rely more heavily on peers and less on the teacher for assistance. This dynamic reinforces the importance of social interaction in classrooms. As a result, student focus is increased, quality relationships are formed, and academic achievement is enhanced (Pelligrini and Blatchford, 2000).

MOTIVATION

Putting together a successful instructional program in the classroom requires a teacher who possesses a philosophy, which promotes positive instruction and feedback between students, and between students and the teacher. Together, positive instruction and feedback produce motivation. Holdaway's (1979) findings indicate that motivation is the act of providing an incentive or reason for doing something. When classroom experiences are meaningful and purposeful, students learn at a higher rate and an elevated level of motivation occurs. Motivation is directly built on finding the level where students succeed and proceeding from that point in a positive direction (Moore, 1999b).

Sometimes motivation comes from within the students; at other times it is fostered by the teacher, classroom atmosphere, or by social and collaborative settings. It is important to note that motivation is not a single activity controlled by the teacher. It involves a complex set of ongoing attitudes and activities that occur in a setting that promotes a classroom culture for learning. Within this environment, students are an active part of their learning. That is, they have opportunities within social settings to practice and manage the strategies that they have been exposed to by the teacher. This development of motivation is critical in creating positive learning experiences and attitudes that will sustain the students' interest and enthusiasm.

USING COLLABORATIVE LEARNING COMMUNITIES TO PROMOTE READING

To illustrate these practices in action, some reading activities will be used as examples. First, after skills for a specific reading task have been taught and the students have a grasp of what they are suppose to learn, ample opportunities for practice needs to be available. One of the methods to accomplish this is through the use of collaborative reading groups. Collaboration is an important feature when a teacher desires to analyze individual developmental differences amongst students in a classroom or period. By using this technique it gives the teacher time to observe or conference with individual students, as needed, during a group's reading time.

Next, the composition of a group should start with one reader who has very good decoding and comprehension skills, and three or four other students. In addition, to the high ability student who is the leader, the other students should be somewhere in the middle ability range. Students in the group receive intrinsic satisfaction because the reading activities are organized in such a way that the skills being taught by the teacher are applied immediately in practice. They take an active part in their educational success, which brings about a form of empowerment. Teachers give group members ample opportunities to apply what they have learned or are learning to solve similar problems amongst themselves, further enhancing empowerment. As active participants in their own learning, they have better opportunities to master and apply previous learned practices to new experiences and circumstances.

STUDENT LEADERS

The leader of the group is responsible for the other members to follow the established guidelines during the reading time. When students are given responsibility in an environment that promotes positive interrelationships, they become a part of the solution. This occurs in part as they learn to be socially responsive and contributors to the motivational, academic, and social outcomes, for their individual group. The expected behavior of each individual member includes; that all in the group stay on task during reading, to offer each other help when sounding out difficult words (1.1), to write down any words that can not be successfully decoded or understood (1.3), and to minimize any excess noise. As students become better readers, they in turn will have a future chance to take on leadership responsibilities, either in the group they are in, or in another newly formed group.

Other examples of academic standards that can be covered during these social/ collaborative reading groups include: (a) 1.1 identifying idioms, analogies, etc., (b) 1.3 identify vocabulary or word meanings, (c) 2.3 cause and effect, (d) 2.4 author's point of view, and (e) 2.6 evidence to support answers.

OTHER SUGGESTIONS FOR ACTIVITIES DURING COLLABORATIVE READING GROUPS

First, determine what specific standards or skills are going to be assessed and how much class time is going to be allowed for the collaborative activity. Second, what other objectives are going to be accomplished? Figure 3.1 is an example of an activity that allows students to work together in a low stress environment to come up with answers as well as students modeling to each other their strategies for comprehending texts. Figure 3.1 also provides guidelines to focus teachers on creating optimal learning environments that foster social relationships, maintain student engagement, and aid in solving academic tasks.

FIGURE 3.1 TEACHER CONSTRUCTED GROUP ACTIVITY

EXAMPLE STANDARDS

Visual and Performing Arts 5th Grade

5.4 Demonstrate social skills that enable students to become leaders/teachers and followers/learners. (Develop rubric on desired social skills, i.e., most desired skills/acceptable skills/skills that need improvement).

English Language Development 3rd-12th Grades

Use decoding skills and knowledge of academic and social vocabulary…(Targeted Vocabulary)

Visual and Performing Arts-Theatre 9th-12th Grade

5.2 Manage time, prioritize responsibilities, and meet completion deadlines…as specified by group leaders; team members, etc. (Create a checklist to be mastered, etc.).

Directions: From the outline below, construct a lesson plan for a collaborative activity. Record the primary purpose of the group assignment, the tasks to be completed, and the process for determining both individual and group accountability when the activity is completed.

Academic standard/purpose: _____

Decisions or social skills to be made:

Number and names of members for each group: _____

Time frames:_____

Have students been taught organizational skills and how to work within a timeframe?

Resources to be used: _____

Are they available in the classroom?

Member roles to be assigned: _____

Behavioral skills to be emphasized: _____

How will it be measured?

Do students understand the requirements completely?

Individual accountability process: _____

How will individual be measured?

Group accountability project: _____

How will group be measured?

Use Assessment Rubrics

Rubrics have already been introduced in the first active teaching strategy (pp. 38-42). In review, rubrics should contain components that identify a quality or performance indicator that is directly related to the academic standard. Rubrics need to be clear, easy for the students to understand, and aligned with the lesson goals.

Other Academic Objectives that can be Implemented in Social Settings

If the academic objectives are centered around using inferences, analyzing, collaboration, evaluating values or applying principles, the following standards could be utilized to demonstrate how this can be a starting point, collaboratively, to master specific academic outcomes.

INFERENCES:

Language Arts/Reading 6th Grade

2.8 Note instances of unsupported inferences, fallacious reasoning, and propaganda in text. (As a group, list them and support findings).

Evaluative task:
Language Arts/Listening and Speaking 9th-10th Grades

2.5 Deliver persuasive arguments, including evaluation and analysis of problems and solutions and causes and effects. (Each member is assigned a specific part of the objective, the individual task collectively accomplishes the group goal).

Collaborative performance:
History-Social Science 11th Grade

Describe the collaboration on legal strategy between African American and white civil rights lawyers to end racial segregation in higher education. (Collaboratively list the strategies and the intended purpose, why was collaboration necessary?)

Visual and Performing Arts 5th Grade

Demonstrate cooperation, collaboration, and empathy in working with partners and in groups (e.g., leading/following, mirroring, calling/responding, echoing, opposing).

Values:
History-Social Science 9th-12th Grades

2. Students analyze how change happens at different rates at different times; understand that some aspects can change while others remain the same; and understand that change is complicated and affects not only technology and politics but also values and beliefs.

3. Students interpret past events and issues within the context in which an event unfolded rather than solely in terms of present-day norms and values.

Principles:
Visual and Performing Arts 5th Grade

4.1 Identify how selected principles of design are used in a work of art and how they affect personal responses to and evaluation of the work of art.

A more complex example for maintaining student engagement by using social and collaborative group settings is demonstrated in Figure 3.2.

FIGURE 3.2 PROOFING THE READING LESSON

EXAMPLE STANDARDS

Language Arts/Reading 5th Grade

2.1 Understand how text features (e.g., format, graphics, sequence, diagrams, illustrations, charts, and maps) make information accessible and usable.

English Language Development:

Identify some significant structural (organizational) patterns in text, such as sequence, chronological order, cause and effect, fact, opinion, and inference.

Directions: Briefly answer each question as it pertains to the reading selection. All in the group will share their answers with each other. Use the summary rubric to assess your work. Finish this activity with a one-sentence summary of what the section was about.

1.   What is the purpose of this assignment? Why am I reading it?
2.   Do I know anything about this story? _____
3.   If so, write a short sentence about what I know. _____
4.   Read the chapter title and any subtitles.
5.   What are they? _____
6.   Read any focus questions at the beginning/end of the chapter.
7.   Read the chapter introduction or first paragraph.
8.   What is it talking about in 3-5 words? _____
9.   Are there any boldface subheadings?
10. List them/their importance. _____
11. Read the first (topic) sentence of each paragraph.
12. Summarize every other paragraph (or other options)._____
13. Identify any visual aids.
14. What are they? _____

15. Read the final paragraph or summary.

16. Why is it important? _____

Assessment Rubric (See previous section on rubric development pp. 38-42). Each section below must be specifically defined a criteria that the students and teacher understand. This objective criterion defines the grade, how it is achieved, and the specific standards needed to receive a grade or value such as an outstanding, satisfactory, or needs improvement.

Point Value or Grade	Number of Titles/Subtitles	Key/Topic Questions	Visual Aids	Write Summary Answers	Other Interesting Points

For figures 3.3 and 3.4, vocabulary development, as well as comprehension skills, is further developed. Figure 3.3 illustrates methods that help promote new vocabulary and words with multiple meanings; whereas figure 3.4 promotes vocabulary, definitions, and words in different context.

FIGURE 3.3 GUIDELINES FOR SELECTING WORDS

EXAMPLE STANDARDS

Language Arts 7th Grade

1.0 Students use their knowledge of word origins and word relationships, as well as historical and literary context clues, to determine the meaning of specialized vocabulary and to understand the precise meaning of grade-level appropriate words.

Visual and Performing Arts 7th Grade

1.2 Discuss a series of original works of art, using the appropriate vocabulary of art.

English Language Development

Use expanded vocabulary and descriptive words and paraphrasing for oral and written responses to text.

Directions: Use selected vocabulary words to guide reading comprehension and vocabulary development. If academic words or grade-approved word lists are used, include them as often as possible in lesson. Select the number of words for the rubric to determine mastery, adequate, or needs improvement.

Rubric

Point Value or Grade	Words on Vocabulary List	Words on Previous Vocabulary Lists	Words Spelled Correctly	Words From Previous Lists Spelled Correctly	Words with Multiple Meanings

- Restrict selection of words to those that are critical to the lesson, concept, comprehension, or the reading selection.

- Choose words that promote academic language use or can be used to define concepts needed for mastery.

- Choose general academic words that students are likely to encounter in various instructional contexts (e.g., aspect, infer, similar, subsequently).

- Choose words that are considered vital for students to master and add to their productive English lexicon.

- Choose words that are likely to be included on a test.

- Choose words that have multiple meanings (e.g., wave: v. to greet or signal versus wave: n. an upsurge or trend, as in a wave of immigrants from Canada).

- Don't spend time reinforcing the meanings of words just because they appear in italics or boldface.

- Don't dwell on low-frequency words that the students are unlikely to encounter.

FIGURE 3.4 READING KNOWLEDGE SHEET I

EXAMPLE STANDARDS

Writing 9ᵗʰ Grade

2.6 Write technical documents that include scenarios, definitions, and examples to aid comprehension.

Reading 8th Grade

1.3 Use word meanings within the appropriate context and show ability to verify these meanings by definition, restatement, example, or comparison.

English Language Development 9th Grade

Use words appropriately that sometimes have multiple meanings and apply this knowledge consistently to literature and texts in content areas.

History/Social Science 6th Grade

6.7.6 Note the origins of Christianity in the Jewish Messianic prophecies, the life and teaching of Jesus of Nazareth as described in the New Testament and the contribution of St. Paul the Apostle to the definition and spread of Christian beliefs.

Directions: If students come across words that you are not sure about, or words that are on the current vocabulary list, please place them on the answer sheet. If students see a new meaning of a word because it has been applied in a different context, please list this word in the new word/context/meaning column.

Rubric

Point Value or Grade	Word	Definition	Heard it/Seen it/ Know it	New word, Context New meaning

TEACHER ASSESSMENT

As groups are working collaboratively, assessment by the teacher can be conducted. This is accomplished by walking around each group, observing and assessing the application of new strategies, listening for reading quality, and monitoring the student's interaction with each other. The authors' have found that by writing anecdotal records or doing a modified running record works quite easily. This is simply done by having index cards taped on a clipboard with the child's name. Two to five students can be easily observed and assessed each time the reading groups are used. This informal assessment demonstrates, in a very authentic and practical way, whether the students have understood the strategies taught, and can apply them successfully.

LESS PROFICIENT READERS

Struggling or less proficient students should read only with the teacher. Usually during the first read through of a story, no assessment of other students in the class can be done; because, the needs of the non-proficient reading group must to be assessed first. However, after the struggling readers have been guided through the text once, they can be assigned a group facilitator for short periods of time so that others can be assessed. Another strategy is to put each of the students from the less proficient reading group into the various other reading groups, for short periods of time.

There are many other ways in which interactive groups can be organized and conducted. The examples used covered many different levels and grades. There is no right or wrong way; if it works for the students and produces a more proficient and focused student, and helps them master grade-level standards, then that's the right way for that specific setting. Five to twenty minutes daily seems to work well in keeping the students on task, depending on grade level and subject matter. Thus, social interaction between teachers and students, interactive group work between students, and student groups interacting with the teacher, enhance, and are important ingredients in keeping the students actively engaged.

INDIVIDUAL ASSESSMENT IN A GROUP ACTIVITY

In addition, a clustering or web activity is another excellent way to evaluate individual learning and keep the students on task during group activities. This can be done in several ways.

- Have students draw a circle in the center of a page with spider legs that connect to other circles, words, sentences, or concept pictures.

- Students have the freedom to web their information in a way that makes sense to them.

- This technique demonstrates how well the students can synthesize information and graphically demonstrate what they have learned.

- Students can also divide a piece of paper into four or eight squares and cartoon/draw out what they have learned in a pictorial format.

In closing the social/collaborative portion of a lesson, a summative group evaluation of activities can be conducted. The students can create their own questions to evaluate the activity, grouping, or grading criteria. This activity can also be created by the teacher. What needs to be gleaned from this type of assessment is:

- How well did the activity go?

- What worked well and why?

- Were their any conflicts?
- What future suggestions can be made to promote academic growth?
- Was the group activity a good use of instructional time? (From the teacher and students perspective).

It needs to be noted that group work and other social and collaboratively responsive strategies should be a small part of a teacher's instructional methods and not constitute the only way that instruction is to be delivered. The examples used in this section were very limited. They were meant to demonstrate a few suggestions and nothing more. It is the outstanding teacher who can create and keep the interaction focused on the academic goals that frames the discussions or groupings in the first place. Many different techniques should be used and changed often to support a child's continual development. In addition, teachers need to strive and create positive relationships with students to help address their social and academic needs. The social or collaborative portion of a student responsive pedagogy has to be built on an academically sound foundation. Without this foundation, socialization occurs without a learning goal or objective that can be legitimatized. If the socialization portion of this model is removed, the academic portion can be reduced to a dry and sterile set of facts, principles, and processes. This makes learning a chore that's lifeless and has no meaning for the students, either in the present, or for their futures.

SUMMARY

To sum up the first two active teaching strategies, which focus on clear communication and maintaining student engagement, teachers need to dialogue with students so that they get the big picture. A basic building block in forming quality classroom relationships is interaction. Positive interaction leads to effective communication, and effective communication builds trust. At some level, students must trust that the teacher cares and can teach them. Teachers continually validate students in various ways by communicating that they are exerting every effort to see the students succeed. Students understand why they are learning something and its purpose, not only in the present, but also information that is a prerequisite for future opportunities.

It needs to be noted that there is a growing body of research that indicates students want to be trusted and respected. They want to be viewed as vital participants in their own learning process. They not only desire teachers who care and help them, but they also want to be held accountable (Weinberger and McCombs, 2003). Through continual engagement, using active teaching strategies, students receive ample guidance, directions, and mentoring. This is essential to their continual academic growth, which is developing in direct proportion to their varied levels of maturity.

CHAPTER 4

ACTIVE TEACHING STRATEGY III: MONITORING OF STUDENT PROGRESS

Piaget's (1973), developmental theory advocates that academic goals should be focused on developing imaginative, innovative, and capable self-regulated students, who take an active part in their educational success. As active participants in their own learning, students have better opportunities to reconstruct previous learned principles to new experiences and circumstances. This practice encourages students to look beyond the answer to understand the process of why a certain response is correct. Students experience a greater level of satisfaction when they feel that they have some say and control over their lives. This leads into the third component of active teaching, the monitoring or overseeing of student progress. The characteristics of the third active teaching strategy are:

- Utilizing cognitive and developmental strategies;
- Observing, monitoring, and reviewing student work on a frequent basis;
- Tailoring learning targets to individual students' needs—process data;
- Adjusting instruction to maximize learning—formative/summative data;
- Evaluate strategy selections;
- Create prescriptive instructional practices

COGNITIVE AND DEVELOPMENTAL STRATEGIES

Over thirty years ago Bonney stated:

A person who has the capacity for learning, for love, or for self-assertion, has at the same time a need to learn, to love, and to be assertive. If these needs are denied or frustrated on a low level, as they often are, the person is denied the completion of his potentials. To the degree that this happens, he becomes apathetic, hostile, or psychologically sick (1969, p. 143).

In relationship to a child's school experience, needs denied can have devastating implications. In the past it has been traditionally assumed that families, specifically the parents, were the curator of a students' learning environment. The parents influenced and prepared the child with a myriad of experiences which were then brought to school. Traditionally these have included the following characteristics:

- Families typically provided an environment of love and support.
- Communication in the home was positive and supportive.
- Family provided safety and security.
- Boundaries and social mores established in the home.
- Family provided appropriate role models.
- Parents had high expectations.
- More quality time spent at home.

CHANGING ROLE OF SCHOOLS

Unfortunately, due to the at-risk conditions that many students are faced with, they are not entering school with traditional backgrounds, or the skills that guides them to enjoy academic success. In fact, schools today are assuming more of this traditional parenting role, which brings about a different type of pressure on the students.

That is, when students learn outside the school environment and fail, the family is there to help and encourage them. However, when these family supports are non-existent in a student's life, a level of shame, or at the least the absence of positive encouragement, brings about frustration, and a sense of hopelessness. The earlier a student experiences these circumstances in school, the greater the possibility that they will become at-risk, or develop a poor attitude towards their education. Currently, more children live in broken homes, take medication, or receive special services than ever before. Although there is less of a stigma, because some of these realities have become commonplace, these factors still effect the students adversely.

Furthermore, because teaching and learning happens at school in a public setting, the major orientation of a student's development should be holistically focused. The student needs to be viewed as an integrated individual, constantly influenced by interacting forces and competing influences. Optimal student growth requires a wide range of social experiences, addressing interpersonal conflicts, maladaptive behavior and the developing value systems of students. Students need freedom to explore, initiate interactions, make mistakes, and to fail under non-threatening conditions. A positive climate needs to be an essential part of the classroom ambiance, conducted within the security of established limits. Additionally, students need the assurance that frequent praise, public recognition, and respect, from both the teacher, and other students, will be the rule, and not the exception. Students are far more likely to blossom and grow in an environment that focuses primarily on their positive assets, instead of those that concentrate on eliminating immature attitudes, behaviors, and academic weaknesses.

THE WHOLE CHILD

When teachers see students holistically, they are attentive to possible problems surrounding student's cognitive and meta-cognitive development, the affective and motivational features of their instructional practices, and the developmental and social aspects of learning. Collectively, these characteristics are addressed with appropriate strategies designed to provide a wide range of activities that are honed to the students developmental and maturity level.

Likewise, preparing students for the future is an increasingly difficult task. All the knowledge, training, and skills needed for teachers to accomplish this does not exist. Therefore, the best that can be done is to help the students learn how to stay motivated and acquire skills that promote lifelong learning. To facilitate this, teachers need to concentrate on developmental activities that promote critical, creative, and intellectual skills, which address all aspects of the students.

According to Woolfolk Hoy, and Tschannen-Moran (1999), as children engage with others who are at different developmental levels and attempt to explain and justify their point of view, they begin to move toward a higher level of development. In the process of learning, students develop new concepts and structures of knowledge. In a similar fashion, Piagetian Theory defines intelligence as the building of various experiences on each other. As students in the classroom encounter something new, they actively work, within their cognitive ability, to relate it to something that they already know. It is this assimilation process, coupled with previous experiences, which triggers the students understanding. If they do not possess the experience or cognitive ability, they must accommodate themselves to finding new solutions.

One of the many reasons that the cognitive and developmental portion of a student-responsive pedagogy is so important, is because each child is truly unique. As students' progress to different grades, their developmental skills and abilities change. These changes are evident in their growth patterns, how they think, speak, and relate to one another. The ramifications of these changes are that teachers' instructional delivery systems need to adapt to this reality and make appropriate and responsive adjustments. If a teacher is not responsive to a student's cognitive and developmental level or needs, optimal learning can be delayed or stymied. Therefore, all students have to be evaluated in terms of what drives them, their academic, social, behavioral, and developmental needs, as well as their feelings.

OBSERVING, MONITORING, REVIEWING

To do this effectively, requires some sort of monitoring of students and their specific academic needs. This process, broadly defined, is about analyzing and monitoring students, academic tasks and the results from those findings and tasks. Monitoring necessitates regular reviewing, refining, and modifying the schooling process to intensify the focus towards the desired results (Schmoker, 1999). Thus, instructional strategies need to evolve from the analysis of student progress. Monitoring the students' strengths and challenges are vital to assess their abilities to make sense of what they are learning and doing. Evaluation of students' strategies, what works and why, need to be examined during this active teaching segment. This allows the teacher to make procedural corrections, re-teach, clarify as needed, encourage students, as well as teach new strategies that will reduce time and promote student success. According to Good and Brophy (2002), student mistakes should be viewed as learning opportunities. This will lead the teacher to clarify instruction, which in turn, will increase comprehension.

By continually monitoring the students, teachers can help choose which method, or combination of methods, are the most beneficial to accomplish a specific task, for a specific student, with specific needs and circumstances. Progression charts, timelines, and anchor papers, used in conjunction with clearly defined rubrics, can help demystify assignments, and help students self-monitor, which keeps them focused to the task at hand.

TAILORED LEARNING TARGETS: UTILIZING PROCESS DATA

To further optimize the monitoring of student progress requires the continual gathering of pertinent information. This information collection, when utilized to bring about a change in a school or classroom culture, which ultimately benefits the student, is called process data. Process data holds the greatest promise in closing the achievement gap between all students. It is an essential necessity for promoting student success because it is the only component over which schools have direct and immediate influence in creating environments that optimizes student learning. This is very important because any child can become at-risk depending on unexpected events that can occur in their life at any given time. Factors that impact process data includes; teacher and administrative expectations about student success, affective pedagogical methods, organization of the curriculum, responsive instructional practices, levels of teacher expertise, equity classroom management, and staffs overall commitment to student success.

Additionally, process data is directly related to classroom or school affect by its influence to impassion the students to learn more. Through monitoring, instructional strategies can be transformed into positive classroom practices. When process data is coupled with other pertinent information gleaned from demographic and formative outcome sources, instructional strategies can be honed to maximize students' academic growth.

WHAT IS FORMATIVE OUTCOME DATA?

Formative data is about "gathering information about learning as learning is taking place, so that 'in flight' instructional modifications may be made to improve the quality and amount of learning" (Anderson, et al., 2001, pp. 101-102). The modification comes as a direct result of the ongoing monitoring of the students.

FIGURE 4.1 FORMATIVE DATA COLLECTION

- How are the students performing in relation to the attainment of academic standards?

- What is not being covered by the current curricular objectives?

- How do I know?

- What can I show as proof that objectives are being mastered?

- Is there a gap between what is being taught versus what students are mastering?

- How am I addressing this gap?

- Is this discrepancy (if applicable) limited to specific students or to the complete class?

- What resources can be made available to remediate any of these identified issues?

- How are teachers ensuring that students' have access to make-up/extra credit work?

- How am I differentiating instruction?

- What resources are available to support proficiency levels of English language learners?

- TITLE I/EIA-LEP/Other sources?

- Do all staff members know the District policy concerning English language learners?

- How are the needs of students with exceptionalities addressed?

- Specifically;
- Blind or visually impaired;
- Learning disabled;
- Deaf or hearing impaired;
- Physically impaired;
- Developmentally disabled;
- Speech impaired;
- Emotionally or behaviorally disabled;
- Other special needs?
- What resources are available to assist students who have exceptionalities?
- What other information is needed to assist teachers with their students?
- What are the student's attitudes toward:
- School in general?
- Learning in particular?
- English as a language (if applicable)?
- What is the students' perception of the English-speaking culture of the United States (If applicable)?
- What is the students' perception about self-efficacy (knowing that the ability to succeed comes from within them)?
- Questioners can be created to find out students opinions that influence their learning?

Figure 4.2 illustrates an example of formative data. It is a standards style language arts test that can be administered several times a year. It gives immediate feedback to the teacher on material that the students are learning, and what information they still need to master at the specific grade level. The results of formative data can be combined with process data to design a framework for student success. Using these two data sources demonstrates how formative assessment, used in the form of a standards-based test, can be utilized to focus curriculum, and program design, (process data) to assess and monitor student growth. Once a baseline has been established, instruction can be modified, and joined with pertinent demographic influences to help all students experience academic success.

FIGURE 4.2 GRADE 7 – EXCERPTS FROM THE LANGUAGE ARTS STANDARDS ASSESSMENT TEST

Spelling

Choose the misspelled word.

1. (WOL 1.7)
   A. easyer
   B. permanent
   C. zipper
   D. reality

2. (WOL 1.7)
   A. hitchhike
   B. oppose
   C. alblum
   D. illegal

3. (WOL 1.7)
   A. effortless
   B. possessed
   C. ultimate
   D. wich

Vocabulary

Use your knowledge of affixes, base words, and roots to help you choose the word that best fits each definition.

(V 1.2)

Which word means "having one shape?"
   A. previewed
   B. reporter
   C. bicolor
   D. uniform

(V 1.2)

Which word means 'to dive beneath?"
   A. permit
   B. reanimate
   C. submerge
   D. transmission

(V 1.2)

Which word means "uneasy, distressed, or awkward?"

A. dominated

B. uncomfortable

C. indomitable

D. dismissed

Select the correct definition of the underlined word in each sentence.
(V1.3)

Unlike his brother and sister, who are slow, Rod is <u>adept</u> at soccer because he is a fast runner.

Adept means:

A. experienced

B. skilled

C. new

D. sensitive

(V 1.3)

For Anna's thirteenth birthday, her mother threw her a <u>lavish</u> party with a live band and ice skating.

Lavish means:

A. clean

B. fun

C. huge

D. late

Punctuation

Choose the letter of the line that includes a mistake in punctuation.
Choose "no mistakes" if everything is correctly punctuated.

6. (WOL 1.4)

   A. "The sky looks as if

   B. it were made of blue silk,

   C. said my dad

   D. when he came inside.

7. (WOL 1.4)

   A. The word complex

   B. came from a Latin word

   C. meaning "to weave."

   D. no mistakes

Read this excerpt and then answer the questions that follow.

(1) Yesterday, Principal Gerber made an announcement that the school day would become thirty minutes longer. (2) There were several reasons for this change more time for class meetings announcements, and longer lunches. (3) Most of the students appeared upset by the news many of the students' relatives were angry as well. (4) When asked, one great grand-mother responded, "She [Principal Gerber] doesn't know what she's doing. (5) My great-granddaughter has ballet after school and she can't be late." ....
(WOL 1.5)

What is the best way to rewrite great grand-mother in sentence 4?
A. great-grand-mother
B. great-grandmother
C. greatgrandmother
D. great, grand mother
(WOL 1.5)

Which sentence contains brackets?
A. sentence 1
B. sentence 3
C. sentence 4
D. sentence 5
(WOL 1.5)

In sentence 3, a semicolon should follow –
A. relatives
B. many
C. news
D. upset

Capitalization
Choose the letter of the line that includes a mistake in capitalization.
Choose "no mistakes" if everything is correctly capitalized.

11. (WOL 1.6)
A. Hurry up! the school bus is
B. ready to leave.
B. no mistakes
C. quartet Pink Floyd
D. Ray Parker Jr.

12. (WOL 1.6)

    A. *Cry, the Beloved Country* is a novel

    B. about race relations by the South African

    C. Author Alan Paton.

    D. no mistakes

13. (WOL 1.6)

    A. After the baseball game,

    B. the boys decided to

    C. go to the city park.

    D. no mistakes

Written and Oral Language (Grammar)

Read each sentence. Look at the underlined words. If there is a mistake in grammar, choose the answer that is the best way to write the underlined section.

If there is no mistake, choose correct as is.

(WOL 1.4 & W 1.7)

<u>As a boy loved</u> to watch the steamboats on the Mississippi River.

    A. As a boy, he loved

    B. A boy who loved

    C. A boy he loved

    D. correct as is

(WOL 1.2)

By the time we arrived, the guests <u>had already started</u> eating dinner.

    A. Has already started

    B. already started

    C. have already started

    D. correct as is

(WOL 1.2)

William wanted <u>to quickly run</u> to the ice cream truck.

    A. quickly to run

    B. to run quickly

    C. to run quick

    D. correct as is

The above portions of the standards assessment test have been matched to the California State Academic Standards for Language Arts in the seventh grade. The test is not meant to be timed so teachers determine whether they wish to give the assessment in one or more sittings. The actual test has been created from a bank of 80 questions. The test contains 60 questions and is designed to give teachers a formative analysis of where their students are in terms of the academic standards that should be learned by the end of the school year. There are typically three items for each of the standards, and some of the items can be classified as more than one standard. The assessment items, with the exception of the individual writing samples, have four answer choices, much as the STAR assessment has. These test items, are not designed to be norm-referenced and are more closely aligned to criterion-referenced items. After students have been assessed on the standards based test, it is scored; the results are then transferred to the matrix shown in figure 4.3.

FIGURE 4.3 EXCERPTS FROM THE SCORING MATRIX FOR STANDARDS BASED ASSESSMENT

Question	Total Count	Total %	Mastery of Standard	Far Below Basic 54.2%	Below Basic 61.6%	Basic 71.9%	Proficient 82.4%	Advanced 82.5%	Standards
17 A*	23	79	0.793				X		**Written & Oral Language/ Grammar**
B	4	14							1.2 identify & use parallelism/similar grammatical forms/ juxtaposes for emphasis
C	0	0							
D	2	7							
18 A	0	0	0.724				X		**Written & Oral Language**
B	4	14							1.1 sentence structure
C	4	14							
D*	21	72							
19 A	1	3	0.759				X		**Written & Oral Language**
B*	22	76							1.2 identify & use parallelism/ similar grammatical forms/juxtapose for emphasis
C	2	7							
D	4	14							
20 A	5	17	0.276	X					**Reading Comprehension/ Informational Material**
B	6	12							2.6 use information from variety of sources to explain/solve problems
C*	8	28							
D	10	34							
21 A	10	34	0.103	X					**Reading Comprehension/ Vocabulary & Concept Develop.**

Rock and Michelle Moore MiRoc Publishing @ AOL.Com

	B*	3	10							1.3 word meanings/context/ definition/ restatement/example/ compare/contrast
	C	7	24							
	D	9	31							
22	A	14	48	0.276	X					**Reading Comprehension/ Informational Material**
	B*	8	28							2.6 use information from variety of sources to explain/ solve problems
	C	5	17							**Literary Response and Analysis**
	D	2	7							3.6 identify literary devices/ metaphor/symbolism/ dialect/irony
23	A*	16	55	0.552		X				**Reading Comprehension/ Informational Material**
	B	6	21							2.6 use information from variety of sources to explain/ solve problems
	C	5	17							**Literary Response and Analysis/ Narrative Analysis**
	D	2	7							3.6 Identify literary devices/ metaphor/symbolism/ dialect/irony
24	A*	19	66	0.655		X				**Literary Response and Analysis/ Narrative Analysis**
	B	1	3							3.5 identify and analyze recurring themes in traditional/contemporary works
	C	2	7							
	D	7	24							
25	A	7	24	0.103	X					**Literary Response and Analysis/ Narrative Analysis**

	B	12	41								3.4 relevance of setting place/ time to mood/ tone and meaning
	C*	3	10								3.6 identify literary devices/ metaphor/ symbolism/ dialect/irony
	D	7	24								
26	A	10	34	0.276	X						**Reading and Vocabulary/ Concept Development**
	B*	8	28								1.1 idioms/analogies/ metaphors/ similes to infer literal/ figurative meaning
	C	9	31								**Literary Response and Analysis/ Narrative Analysis**
	D	2	7								3.6 identify literary devices/ metaphors/ symbolism/dialect/irony
27	A	3	10	0.446	X						**Reading Comprehension/ Informational Material**
	B	31	9								1.1 similarities/differences between text in treatment/ scope/ organization
	C*	13	45								**Reading Comprehension/ Expository Critique**
	D	4	14								2.7 evaluate unity/ coherence/logic/ internal consistency/patterns
28	A	11	38	0.103	X						**Reading Comprehension/ Analysis**
	B*	3	10								1.1 compare original text to summarize/ accurately captures main ideas
	C	8	28								**Reading Comprehension/ Expository Critique**

Rock and Michelle Moore MiRoc Publishing @ AOL.Com

	D	7	24							1.1 evaluate unity/ coherence/logic/ internal consistency/patterns
29	A	15	52	0.172	X					**Reading Comprehension/ Structural Features**
	B*	5	17							1.1 analyze text that uses proposition and support patterns
	C	6	21							**Literary Response and Analysis/ Narrative Analysis**
	D	3	1							3.4 relevance of setting place/time to mood/ tone and meaning
30	A	3	10	0.069	X					3.4 identify and analyze recurring themes in traditional/ contemporary works
	B	10	24							**Writing Strategies/ Organization and Focus**
	C	14	48							1.1 create compositions/ controlled impression/ coherent/clear
	D*	7	2							
31	A	4	14	0.172	X					**Reading and Vocabulary/ Concept Development**
	B	4	10							1.1 word meanings/definition/ restatement/example/ compare/contrast
	C	17	59							
	D*	5	17							
32	A	11	38	0.552		X				**Reading Comprehension/ Structural Features**
	B*	16	55							2.2 analyze text that uses proposition and support patterns
	C	1	3							
	D	1	3							2.4 compare original text to summarize/accurately captures main idea

The Standards Matrix has been matched to the academic standards test and was created by the authors. The first column (Left-Right) is the question that corresponds to the test. The letter with the asterisk is the correct response. The total count column is the number of students who answered a particular selection. Next, is the total percentage column of students who answered a particular response. Mastery of standards is tabulated between 0-1000. A zero means little or no understanding, whereas a 1000 would demonstrate mastery of a standard being used in a particular application. The next five columns are cut scores that correspond with the CAT-6 assessment. When the CAT-6 is returned to the school, the students' total score is placed into one of these cut score boxes, which indicates a students' level of proficiency. This matrix duplicates the state standards STAR format and utilizes a common language.

With the utilization of formative data like the standards test, coupled with process and demographic information (Chapter 1), a student specific blueprint can be appropriately created to further monitor and optimize learning. This blueprint employs student specific home and background information, special circumstances, and any other pertinent facts with a set of effective instructional strategies designed to monitor students' progress. These plans and strategies, when put into practice, have the greatest chance of monitoring as well as promoting student growth. In addition, these goals become the essential ingredients to take all students to their at-promise potential.

ADJUSTING INSTRUCTION TO MAXIMIZE LEARNING: UTILIZING FORMATIVE DATA

All data needs to be evaluated in ways that monitors student growth. Without this scrutiny and thoroughness in analyzing the data, valuable insight into the lives of the students will be lost. Worst yet, if assessments have been conducted and the information has not been viewed critically, it will never produce the desired outcome or result.

For students to reach their potential, a shift in thinking is required by both teachers and administrators. This collaborative effort, through the implementation of process data, is committed to change in several specific areas. These areas include at a minimum, planning, focus, philosophy, and the continual monitoring of data. This data dissemination brings about a wealth of knowledge about the students' lives, how they live, what is important to them, things they like and dislike, and possible obstacles to their learning. For teachers, this information is crucial in making positive connections and forming relationships with the students. These relationships directly influence student interest as well as their academic achievement. Implementing information about students requires teachers to know exactly what their targeted goals are academically, socially, and behaviorally, and to monitor those goals continually.

This monitoring of student data becomes an essential component of the teachers' classroom methodology. Figure 4.4 graphically sums up the various data sources that can be monitored to optimize student success.

FIGURE 4.4 GRAPHIC SUMMARIES OF DATA

Summative Data Information gathered after learning has occurred *SAT 9   CAT 6*
Demographic Data Understanding the uniqueness of all students *Students Staff Schooling History Community*
Process Data Creating environment for student success *Expectations Attitudes Curriculum*
Formative Data Information gathered about learning as learning is taking place *Standards/Content Test   Authentic/ Performance Assessment*

Other ways of assessing and analyzing data concerning students' attainment and progress towards academic standards can be evaluated through

- Various informal classroom observations;
- Teacher-made tests coupled with classroom generated-rubrics;
- Standards based formative tests that are site/district specific;
- Authentic performance assessments;
- Standards-based outlines for writing, e.g., contextualization;
- Defining topics, audience, etc.

Through the use of formative, process, summative, and demographic data, teachers can tailor their instructions to communicate effectively the academic goals in an affective environment that emphasizes the importance of the student as a learner, a human being, an important contributor, and a valued member of society. The monitoring process focuses on the students as unique individuals, and not as a number, in a classroom of 20-40.

UNIQUE DIFFERENCES

The wide range of individual differences [students possess] surely must mean that there is no single method for nurturing creativity; ideally the experiences we provide should be tailor-made, if not for individual students, at least for different types of students. We must remember that the same fire that melts the butter hardens the egg (MacKinnon, 1978, p. 171).

Evaluating and analyzing issues surrounding a student's developmental and cognitive needs directs the focus on to students and not solely on the subject matter taught. Two important aspects of this focus are language development and learning. These are fundamental issues because a classroom is, in reality, a group of individuals who are at different developmental and cognitive levels; learning at differentiating rates.

PRESCRIPTIVE INSTRUCTIONAL PRACTICES

It is a fact that thinking and learning are individual processes. Therefore, instructional strategies need to be prescriptive in relation to the student's individual backgrounds and the specific skills that they currently possess, as well as those needed to master academic outcomes. It is important to point out that learning to learn is not the same as teaching one to read, write, or spell for the first time. Learning how to learn involves motivation and finding pleasure in accomplishing and understanding activities. It consists of engaging in purposeful action with a specific objective or goal in mind.

Likewise, learning relies heavily on the development and comprehension of language. Nothing in language exists outside of its context, making language an essential component of the communication and learning process. The more complex the instruction, the more facts that are required; the more facts, the more clues, the more clues, the better the understanding. This dynamic process can not be accomplished without comprehension, and comprehension can only occur through the language and vocabulary that is being used to input the knowledge and information.

It needs to be pointed out that language is much more than the collection of sounds or words; it is the essential foundation for exchanging information, opinions, advice, and evaluating tasks. Language helps learners regulate their behavior; communicate with others, and negotiate what they need from their environment. Nearly three million students enrolled in school speak a language other than English at home. For many of these students, their language skills in English comprehension are limited (Borich and Tombari, 1997).

SECOND LANGUAGE LEARNERS

Second language students need specially designed props and classroom instruction to facilitate their language learning. These students need to be exposed and make use of a number of variables such as task expectations, role differences, and previous utterances from classroom discourse to formulate their interpretations, and thereby learn. They are typically challenged in situations where they must be understood, and in turn be understood by others, to have their academic, social, and contextual needs met. Halliday (1985) established that in any meaningful language event, students need opportunities to learn language, learn about language, and learn through language. They receive opportunities to use their communicating skills by listening to fluent speakers, trying to talk at whatever their proficiency level allows, and by practicing the language through classroom lessons. This research states that these aspects of language learning function only in a meaningful context; which includes the social, contextual, and individual processes.

Furthermore, the students' construction of knowledge is both shaped and constrained by the language and tools available in social and cultural contexts. Thus, teachers need to identify the students' current level of proficiency, monitor their problem solving skills, and utilize scaffolds to facilitate language growth and reinforce comprehension.

INSTRUCTIONAL SUPPORTS

Scaffolding, in general, is a set of strategies intended to reduce the amount of time needed to master a task. Its purpose is to give students support mechanisms that help them go beyond their current demonstrative levels. Scaffolds are meant to be temporary to help students' complete tasks and to stay motivated. The significance of this is of utmost importance in demonstrating an English learners' developmental and cognitive level of achievement. One can be gifted in their primary language, but can not demonstrate these same qualities through the English language, because of their low level of proficiency. Therefore, using scaffolds are an excellent instructional strategy because it helps reduce the time it takes to acquire adequate proficiency. Some suggested activities include:

- Using the students' background knowledge;
- pre-teaching necessary vocabulary and academic vocabulary;
- refer to the vocabulary often and vary its use in context;
- use visuals (pictures, overheads, realia, charts) to explain concepts;
- have students write/discuss their understanding of concepts with class to reinforce comprehension;

- use study guides, graphic organizers, outlines, and cartooning strategies;

- modify presentation (speak clearly, repeat often, repeat content specific principles or concepts, reinforce academic vocabulary, and continually vary sentence styles and lengths);

- modify the techniques for language arts (integrate reading, writing, speaking and listening in lessons);

- model, demonstrate, and check for understanding continually in smaller increments;

- provide immediate opportunities to practice directly after modeling and demonstrating;

- use a variety of learning modes (interactive, contextualization, hands-on, group projects);

- use a variety of assessment methods; and

- assign independent work.

INSTRUCTIONAL SCAFFOLDS

As previously stated, scaffolds are support mechanisms that aid students in helping them move beyond their current demonstrative levels, which are hampered due to the lack of English language or academic proficiency. Second language and other at-risk learners need several scaffolds for each assignment to demonstrate their level of understanding and increase their proficiency.

FIGURE 4.5 SCAFFOLDS

Modeling: Shows students the steps in getting the assignment completed. It involves the teacher completing a task or using a strategy so students can observe and build a cognitive and conceptual map of the steps required to accomplish something specific. The teacher walks the students clearly and precisely through each step so that the students understand. Samples of finished products and rubrics are helpful in illustrating what is expected in reference to a standard.

Bridging: Involves the students on a personal basis; makes instruction relevant through personal experience and prior knowledge. This is another example of where the teachers have successfully gleamed student data and reaped the benefits.

Schema-building: Involves clustering interrelated concepts by showing interconnectedness, i.e., chronological order, sequencing, and story maps. In addition, it utilizes graphic organizers to compare/contrast, cluster concepts, Venn diagrams, and webbing, all of which reinforces student understanding.

Meta-cognitive development: Knowing how one knows; knowing, planning and assessing to demonstrate acquired knowledge. Teacher can demonstrate to students how thinking occurs through reciprocal teaching, think-alouds, etc.

Contextualization: Creating environments through the use of one or more senses to make content meaningful. Teacher uses personal experience, students' prior knowledge, pictures, and other sensory clues, to facilitate comprehension. Delivery of instructional material to students is in context and not separate from it.

Text re-presentation: The transformation of text (oral, written, visual, etc.) to demonstrate understanding by the use of an alternative format. Use of cooperative dialogues between students, the presentation of a story in an alternative format or creative twist, demonstrates comprehension of materials read.

FIGURE 4.6 TURNING SCAFFOLDS INTO INSTRUCTIONAL PRACTICES

When using scaffolds, it is a good practice to isolate the activities into three different components, with each serving a different purpose. The first, "priming the pump" gets the students ready for the activities. Second, "engaging students" involves isolating task and standards to accomplish specific task. Lastly, "making connections" helps the students put what they are learning into context, and helps them in the generalization process. The practices below serve as a starter list for these types of scaffolding activities.

Priming the Pump: Prepares students for understanding a lesson and the corresponding academic standards.

- Clues from book title/chapter; **Reading Standard 2.3, 4th grade. Make/ confirm predictions.**

- Anticipatory guides/charts; **Reading Standard 2.1, 5th grade. Understand how charts, illustrations, diagrams make information accessible and usable**.

- Advanced organizers; **Science Standard 6g, 5th grade. Record data by using appropriate graphic representations (including charts, graphs, and labeled diagrams and make inferences based on the data.**

- Video/sound clips; **Writing Standard 2.3, 11th grade. Students draw information from television, videos, films, etc**.

- Focus questions/conversations; **English Language Development. Negotiate and initiate social conversations by questioning, restating, soliciting information and paraphrasing.**

- Background knowledge/visualization; **Listening and Speaking Standard 1.4, 7th grade. Organize information to achieve particular purposes and to appeal to the background and interest of those involved.**

Engaging Students: Supports students while engaged in the assignment.

- Working with text coherence: mapping, outlining, jigsaw, or readings; **Writing Standard 1.3, 7th grade. Use strategies of note taking, outlining, and summarizing.**

- Think aloud; **Visual and Performing Arts Standard 5.4, 6th grade. Describe orally tactics employed in advertising to sway the viewer's thinking and provide examples.**

- Reciprocal teaching; **Listening and Speaking Standard 1.1, 3rd grade. Retell, paraphrase, and explain what has been said by a speaker.**

- Anticipating developments; **Investigating and Experimentation Standard 6d, 4th grade. Conduct multiple trials to test a prediction and draw conclusions about the relationships between predictions and results.**

- Strip story/cartooning; **Investigating and Experimentation Standard 4d, 2nd grade. Write or draw descriptions of a sequence of steps, events, and observations.**

- Paraphrase; **Written and Oral Language Standard 1.5d, 9th grade. Integration of source and support material (e.g., use of direct quotes and paraphrasing) for oral and written responses to texts.**

- Character analysis; **English Language Development. Discuss stories in greater detail including the characters, plot, summary, and their perceptions about each.**

- Identifying sources; **Writing Standard 2.3, 6th grade. Write reports with facts, details, examples and explanations from multiple authorities sources (e.g., speakers, periodicals, bibliographies, and online sources.**

Making Connections: These are activities meant to help students through context, personal experience, and prior knowledge. Making connections are about (1) application, (2) creativity, (3) reflection, and (4) self-assessment.

- Matching texts and diagrams;

- match several texts to corresponding diagrams;

- match one text to several diagrams;

- select several texts and apply to one diagram;

- select one text and label an unlabeled diagram;

- label a diagram with a set of statements;

- decide which statements one agrees with;
- diagrams of process in sequence and sentences describing the same process in disorder, arrange correct diagram in proper order;
- making inferences;
- extracting information;
- inserting information;
- summarizing;
- problem solving;
- comparing different texts about the same incident;
- writing options;
- changing the genre: from prose to dialogue;
- from poetry to prose;
- from dialogue to narrative; and
- narrative to diary entry, etc.

Strategies involving scaffolding requires a large amount of time, which can and does demand sensitivity to time constraints. However, outstanding teachers know that without these methods the students, second language learners, as well as others who are high risk, are short changed because their levels of comprehension are greatly diminished. As a result of not comprehending, they are, in essence, failing to learn. The trade-off is either to teach mastery of a standard in depth or have students exposed to many standards for breath.

LEARNING RATES

Concerning the amount of time needed for mastery; Carroll's (1963) findings indicate that learning equals time on task over the time needed to learn a task (learning = time/learn). That is, learning is based on two conditions: the amount of time it takes for a student to learn something, and the amount of time a student actually needs to be on task to master a specific learning goal, strategy, or objective. The importance of this is; if the time it takes to master academic objectives are reduced, then students can learn more. That is, the learning curve is shortened through the use of continual monitoring, scaffolds, and data dissemination. In addition, classroom context (Chapter 5) enhances the learning because there are ample opportunities to understand and apply immediately what is being learned at a deeper level of understanding (Branford, Brown, and Cocking 1999).

The premise of Carroll's model is that the degree of school learning is a function of the time a student actually spends on the learning, relative to the time the student needed to spend to achieve proficiency. Likewise, Carroll proposed that aptitude should be defined as the amount of time needed to reach prescribed academic levels, and he called this a students' learning rate. Students would not be labeled as those who were good or poor learners, but as those who were either fast or slow in their ability to comprehend and apply what they were being taught.

Other factors that Carroll's model addressed included the significant relationship between what the students were being taught, and the quality of instruction being delivered. Guskey (1980) further researched this connection and surmised that if quality classroom instruction could be delivered to the students, and they were given ample opportunities to learn, that as many as 95% of the students could be expected to learn and attain mastery. Twenty years later, Raths (2002) findings concur with Carrolls. That is:

1.   If the amount of learning that takes place in a class increases…one [can] infer that instruction has improved.

2.   If students increase their time on task within a lesson or unit of study…one can [infer] that instruction has improved.

3.   If the time students need to learn objectives of a lesson or unit is reduced because of scaffolding…one [can] infer that instruction has improved.

4.   If the complexity of the objectives addressed increases across lessons or units…one [can] infer that instruction has improved.

5.   If the activities assigned to students and the assessments given to students are more closely aligned with a lesson's or unit's objectives…one [can] infer that instruction has improved (pp. 233-234).

Meaningful learning takes place when students can achieve deep understanding of what has been taught. They need time to think and reflect about what they are learning. If they have comprehended the instruction, at their appropriate cognitive and developmental levels, they will be able to paraphrase, draw inferences, and apply principles learned to other subject areas, precisely as Carroll theorized.

EVALUATE STRATEGY SELECTIONS

Another practice to monitor student progress is to evaluate their strategy choices and how they choose to get a task done. The model below can be used to accomplish this investigative process and further monitor student growth.

FIGURE 4.7 THE 3P 2E MODEL FOR MONITORING STRATEGY USAGE

EXAMPLE STANDARDS

Reading Standards 4th Grade.

2.2 Use appropriate strategies when reading for different purposes (e.g., full comprehension, location of information, personal enjoyment, etc.).

Listening and Speaking/Writing Standards 7th Grade.

2.1c Students use a range of strategies (e.g., dialogue, suspense, naming of specific narrative action, including movement, gestures, and expression.

Mathematical Reasoning 6th Grade.

2.0 Students use strategies, skills, and concepts in finding solutions.

Visual and Performing Arts Standards 5th Grade.

Invent multiple possibilities to solve a given movement problem and analyze problem solving strategies and solutions.

Directions: Use this model as a guide to evaluate students' learning strategies. It can be adapted in many ways to facilitate and accelerate meaningful learning.

PI—Preparation/Prompt

Students demonstrating what strategies they know and can use -- This step helps students keep track of the steps they use when solving a problem. This practice develops student's meta-cognitive awareness and self-knowledge through activities such as:

- Discuss what strategies students are familiar with and are already using for specific academic tasks;

- Use and share strategy questionnaires in which students indicate the frequency with which they use particular strategies for particular tasks; and

- Individual think-aloud in which the student works on a task and describes his/her rational as they describe each step in a specific problem solving sequence.

PII—Presentation

Teacher illustrating alternative or modified strategies. When modeling a strategy, teachers are not teaching students what to do, but how to think (Dorn and Soffos, 2001).

Teach the strategy explicitly by:

- Model how the strategy is used with a specific academic standard. This is accomplished by the teacher thinking aloud and working through a task (e.g., reading a text or writing a paragraph);

- Give the strategy a name and refer to it consistently by that name;

- Explain to students how the strategy will help them learn the material quicker and more efficiently; and

- Describe when, how, and for what kinds of standards this strategy is the most useful, and the reasoning behind its use.

- Identify strategies that are ineffective or time consuming that hinder instead of helping students' success.

It needs to be noted that in the PI phase, the students shared their plan of attack to accomplish their assignments. This demonstrated their level of meta-cognitive awareness of their possible choices, as well as their limitations in their strategy use. The PII phase has the teacher demonstrating different ways to increase the students' repertoire of methods to gain mastery of the standard, principle, topic, or practice being learned. Thus, the first, generated by students, shows what they are aware of, the second, generated by the teacher, demonstrates a larger field of strategies, which are more time effective, to help optimize learning.

PIII—Practice

Provide many opportunities for strategy practice through activities such as: Individual

- Provide ample time for refection on task

- Keep various journals describing accomplishments, how to do assignments

- List goals, keep timelines, evaluate progress through self monitoring

- Mentally compute equations

- Listen to a book on tape

    Collaborative Learning

- Work cooperatively with others on various tasks

- Play various team games

- Measure various objects together

- Discuss current/controversial topic in a group setting

    Reciprocal Teaching

- Interview classmates

- Rewrite stories with a partner with alternative endings
- Take turns collaboratively solving disputes
- Create various patterns with manipulatives

Hands-on assignments or experiments

- Solve math problems with manipulatives
- Play checkers/other board games
- Play chess
- Draw map of a specific location
- Make a diorama
- Paint/draw pictures to depict a story
- Create a poster about thoughts on a current event
- Do various schematic drawings
- Put together jigsaw sentences/words
- Solve a maze

Mathematics word problems

- Do word problem brain teasers
- Make graphs from word problems
- Make something following a recipe
- Solve analogies
- Create math journal on solving problems

Research projects

- Conduct a scientific experiment
- Compare and contrast several different theories

Developing oral and written reports

- Write poetry
- Write a journal/diary
- Participate in a debate
- Give a dramatic reading
- Write a sequel to a story

Active Teaching and Learning Strategies
Creating a Blueprint for Success

- Create classroom newspaper
- Write and give a persuasive speech

Analyzing literature

- Retell a story to someone else
- Pretending to question the author
- Analyzing what is author trying to say
- Why is the author telling us that?; (c)

Process writing

- Listing five parts of a story: setting, purpose, action, conclusion, and emotions of the characters in story (Beck, Mckeown, Hamilton, and Kucan, 1997; Graham, Harris, and Reed, 1992).

EI—Evaluation

The focus is on process and not the end result. Method develops students' metacognitive awareness of which strategies work for them-and why-through self-evaluation activities such as:

- Debriefing discussions after using strategies;
- Learning logs or journals in which students describe and evaluate their strategy use in step by step details;
- Comparing their own performance on a task completed without using learning strategies and a similar task in which they applied strategies;
- Checklists of their degree of confidence in using specific strategies;
- Self-efficacy questionnaires about their degree of confidence in completing specific academic tasks; and
- Self-reports telling when they use or do not use a strategy, and why.

EII—Expansion

Provides for transfer of strategies to new tasks through activities such as:

- Scaffolding, in which reminders to use a strategy are gradually diminished;
- Praise for independent use of a strategy;
- Self-report in which students bring tasks to class on which they have successfully transferred a strategy;
- Demonstrate to others how they can use strategy;

- Thinking skills discussions in which students brainstorm possible uses for strategies they are learning;

- Follow-up activities in which students apply the strategies to new tasks and contexts;

- Analysis and discussion of strategies individual students find effective for particular tasks;

- Builds communication skills because students can not only comprehend what they have done but can communicate process effectively to others.

ORGANIZATIONAL SKILLS

Another technique for monitoring student strategy use is through the use of time-lines and evaluating other organizational skills. Figure 4.8 illustrates an example of a two-week timeline. However, these outlines can be adapted to any time frame and serves as an important point of reference for students to learn and stay on task.

FIGURE 4.8 EXAMPLE TIMELINE OUTLINE

Directions: Have class write down key task that must be finished to bring about a successful completion of a lesson, unit, or project.

Day-1   Determine exactly what the assignment is and identify due date.

Day-2-4 Project Preparation: read, research, and gather assigned materials.

Day-5   Summarize reading material by answering: who, what, where, when, how, why.

Day-6   Preliminary project/task make revisions as needed.

Day-11   Project construction: lay out, prepare all materials.

Day-12   Touch up, label, revise, check that all items are included for academic task.

Day-13   Write paragraph from summary (Day 5).

Day-14   Turn completed assignment in.

(McCarney, Wunderlish, Bauer, 1993, p. 498).

To monitor what students are learning in reference to what is being taught, a double column form or "T" notes can be utilized. This exercise can also be used as a study guide for students or as a graded assignment for teachers. Assessment can be performed on sentence structure, complete ideas, punctuation, thoroughness of answers, etc. As students master these types of organizational skills, it facilitates the deeper acquisition of active learning strategies.

FIGURE 4.9 DOUBLE-COLUMN FORM SAMPLE

EXAMPLE STANDARDS

History-Social Science 6th Grade

1. Students frame questions that can be answered by study and research.

Visual and Performing Arts 9th Grade

Create projects for studying in other school courses that involve film, video, and other electronic media.

Directions: The teacher list on the left side of the paper a series of questions to guide students in their comprehension, organization, and mastery of material. The students answer on the right hand side of their paper the correct responses to what information is being gleamed from a given lesson.

Study Guide (Teacher Generated)	The Santa Fe Trail (Student Generated)
Who used the Santa Fe trail?	Settlers used the Santa Fe Trail.
What was the Santa Fe Trail?	The Santa Fe Trail was a trade route.
Where did the Santa Fe Trail go?	The Santa Fe trail went from Independence, Missouri to Santa Fe, New Mexico.
When did the Santa Fe Trail begin?	The trail began in the 1820's.
How did the settlers travel?	The settlers traveled on prairie schooners.
Why was the Santa Fe Trail used?	Settlers used the Santa Fe Trail to move West and for trading purposes.

(McCarney, Wunderlish, Bauer, 1993).

Techniques that utilize timelines, study guides, or any other individualized study helps are useful to monitor students' growth in relationship to specific academic tasks. As these student skills are honed and internalized, four fundamental life skills start to germinate:

- Time management and organizational planning,
- ability to comprehend, summarize, and take both mental and physical notes,
- test-taking strategies and preparation practices, and
- the ability to communicate effectively through written, speaking, or oral techniques.

These example-monitoring practices guide the students to skills that break down their assignments into smaller, attainable, and more manageable segments. Conversely, if a deadline for a project or assignment is missed or a test score represents a poor showing of effort, alternative strategies are revisited with the student to promote their success. What is important to note here is that it is the strategy, not the student, that is being addressed. By using these guidelines, students gain a greater sense of control, build confidence, and are less likely to feel overwhelmed by classroom activities.

When teachers are actively monitoring students and providing them with tasks that are both challenging and meaningful, they learn to master the academic standards. Monitoring of work helps students build confidence in themselves, their initiative, and their ability to take risk.

CHAPTER 5

ACTIVE TEACHING STRATEGY IV: IMMEDIATE FEEDBACK

Good feedback is essential for student success. Equally important, positive feedback lowers anxiety and promotes motivation. In addition, it provides many opportunities for corrective alternatives, suggested by the teacher, or others, to be employed. This is the essence of the fourth active teaching strategy. It is characterized by providing immediate feedback and teaching in context. This helps students by giving them access to strategies and information that will guide them to successful outcomes. The purpose of the fourth active teaching strategy is to:

- **Provide immediate feedback,**
- **Promote contextual strategies,**
- **Give positive praise, and**
- **Bring about further academic refinement and improvement.**

Providing students with immediate feedback guides them to new and improved strategies for their individual success. It also promotes a catalyst for student ownership and motivation. Immediate feedback also increases self-efficacy, due in part to the students attributing the positive feedback to their own efforts and hard work (Chapter 6), (Schunk, 1983; 1987).

PROVIDE IMMEDIATE FEEDBACK

Teachers interact and communicate with students so that they understand and get the big picture of what is being taught and why. Teachers continually demonstrate how skills learned in school have direct application to the students' future. This brings about a high level of buy-in and motivation. Students learn optimally when they understand that what is presented to them has some significance in their lives. Learning activities need to be organized for students in such a way that individual facts, processes, and principles are taught within the larger context of what is expected to be mastered, at a certain grade level, or within some established academic standard.

CONTEXTUALIZATION STRATEGIES

When feedback is not immediate, or the understanding of materials by the students is assumed, the results can be disastrous. To illustrate, the author recalls spending a month teaching a third grade lesson on the history of the United States. This particular section was on the "Plain States" and the chapters title was "A Sea of Green." After many hours of teaching the material and having students take several tests and quizzes, the unit ended. One of the students came up and asked about the water, where was the sea of green located? In other words, the student had not made the connection between the grasslands (figuratively, the sea) that went on for hundreds of miles, to the reference that it looked like an ocean of grass (comprehension). This was a valuable lesson concerning context. If a student lacks understanding and does not comprehend what has been taught, then it would be correct to state that the student did not learn the delivered material.

Another example is from teaching and using nouns. During a lesson, students were asked about the nation's capitol located in Washington D.C. During review, when students were asked what a noun was, they replied the definition they had memorized, that a noun is a person, place, or object. The question then:

When talking about the nation's capital, is Washington D.C. a noun?

Students reply: Don't know.

Question: Is it a noun?

Students reply: Don't know?

Question: What is a noun?

Students reply: Person, place, or object.

Question: Is Washington, D.C. a person, place, or object?

Students reply: Not sure.

Incidents like these occur frequently in many classrooms, and at all grade levels daily. One of the reasons is lack of clear communication and an understanding of context delivered by the teacher to the students. In essence, oral communication in a classroom involves a sender (teacher) and a receiver (students). Unfortunately this process of delivering and receiving information is not that clean or simple. When information is imparted to students, it is assumed that they receive it in the way it was meant to be delivered, resulting in comprehension. This assumption however has some serious flaws. When any information is delivered, it is filtered through students various levels of understanding. These levels include comprehension of language, vocabulary context, past experiences, and comfort levels. Pressley and Wharton-McDonald (1997) found that in a similar classroom assignment on nouns, students explained that the purpose of learning nouns was so they could underline them on their answer sheets. This is why feedback and the contextualization of classroom materials are so important.

When working with context, students need to be able to organize information or recall previous learned information and use it in different settings. They also need to have opportunities to immediately apply what they have just learned.

READING EXCERPT I

Figure 5.1 demonstrates one way to use context for teaching nouns. In addition, this practice supports meaningful learning, and provides a chance for students to receive immediate feedback.

> *Barbara Jordan's resume is a catalog of accomplishments: the first African American woman elected to the Texas State Senate, the first African American woman from the South elected to the U.S. Congress, and a recipient of the Presidential Medal of Freedom. By applying her characteristic persistence and well-honed oratorical skills, Jordan triumphed over challenges and earned the respect of the nation.*
>
> *Jordan was born in Houston, Texas, in 1936, during the Great Depression. Her family of seven lived in a two-bedroom home in one of Houston's poorest neighborhoods. Jordan's parents encouraged her to work hard, get good grades, and speak clearly and articulately…*

FIGURE 5.1 NOUNS

Directions: Have students write down every noun that they discover. List the nouns as a person, place, object, and whether the noun is a proper one or not. Any word that students are not sure of, please list in the not sure column.

EXAMPLE STANDARDS

Grammar 2nd Grade

1.3 Identify and correctly use various parts of speech, including nouns, verbs, in writing and speaking.

Capitalization 2nd Grade

1.6 Capitalize all proper nouns.

(Please see previous rubric developments on pages 28-32).Rubric

Point Value or Grade	Word	Proper Noun	Place	Object/Thing	Not Sure
	Barbara Jordan	Xx			
	Debate team				Xx
	Freedom Medal	Xx		Xx	
	Houston, TX	Xx	Xx		
	House of Representatives				Xx

The above exercise can be modified in many ways depending on the academic goals. Using the same article on Barbara Jordan, the lesson's focus can be changed to serve a different purpose, or teach another concept in context. For example students can distinguish between; nouns, verbs, and adverbs, and isolate and remediate any confusion as it arises.

FIGURE 5.2 WORD ROOTS

Directions: After reading the above selection, locate and write down all forms of the given root word in its noun, verb, adverb, and adverb form.

EXAMPLE STANDARDS

Vocabulary and Concept Development 4th Grade

1.3 Know common roots and affixes derived from Greek and Latin.

English Language Development

Read inflectional forms (e.g., -s, -ed, -ing) and root words (e.g., looked, looking).

Rubric

Point Value or Grade	Word	Noun	Verb	Adjective	Adverb

Using the same format but with different standards, this assignment can be changed to one that identifies words that have multiple meanings.

FIGURE 5.3 MULTIPLE MEANING WORDS

Directions: Decide how well students know these multiple meaning words by checking and assessing their knowledge for each.

EXAMPLE STANDARDS

Reading 6th Grade

1.2 Identify and interpret figurative language and words with multiple meanings.

English Language Development

Recognize that words sometimes have multiple meanings and apply this knowledge to literature and text in content areas.

Rubric

Point Value or Grade	Word	Heard It/Seen It Know It	Identify Multiple Meaning Words	Define Multiple Meaning Words

READING EXCERPT II

Figure 5.4 demonstrates another way to use a reading assignment to keep students engaged when learning homophones and homographs in context.

The wild mules of Rocague (Roc-a-hee), an island off the coasts of Maryland and Virginia, walk along the beaches and wander through saltwater marshes. They search for beach grasses among the trees and bushes. They have never felt a rider on them, worn a bridle, or slept in a barn.

How the mules came to be on the island remains a mystery. According to one legend, the mules were left on the island by people who took them there to feed on the grasses. Another popular legend says that the mules arrived on a Russian ship. When the ship went down in a storm, the mules managed to reach the island's shore and stayed there. Yet another legend claims the mules were left behind by pirates who used the island for a while as their temporary home. Regardless of which legend is true, the mules have been grazing on the island for about 300 years.

FIGURE 5.4 WORD SEARCH

Directions: Decide how well students know these words by checking their knowledge for each. Be sure to mark all columns that apply.

EXAMPLE STANDARDS

Vocabulary and Concept Development for 5th Grade

1.3 Understand and explain frequently used synonyms, antonyms, and homographs.

English Language Development

Demonstrate internalization of English grammar, usage, and word choice by recognizing and correcting errors when speaking or reading aloud.

Rubric

Point Value or Grade	Word	Definition	Heard It/Seen It/ Know It	New Word/ New Meaning	Example
	Homophone				Do
	Homograph				Live
	Word with Prefix				Uninhabited
	Multiple Meaning				Raise
	Word with Suffix				Regardless

In figures 5.1, through 5.4 students are able to read and see relationships between text and the assessment of what they are learning. These four examples covered nouns, root words, multiple meaning words, homographs, and homophones. The students are also able to receive immediate feedback that tells them about what they are learning and how well they understand the information. This set of practices immediately lowers students' level of anxiety, and increases their motivation to learn. In these examples contextualization accelerates the learning and comprehension process because there is very little time between presentation and assessment.

In figure 5.5 a pre-reading guide is provided for the students to use. This guides students who may not be well organized, or those who have not learned how to systematically acquire information in an efficient or effective manner. This is a valuable vehicle for information about the students understanding and is another way to provide immediate feedback to the teacher.

FIGURE 5.5 PRE-READING GUIDE

Directions: Please use the following guide to assist you in gaining an overview of the following reading assignment.

EXAMPLE STANDARDS

World History 7th Grade

7.11.4 Explain how the main ideas of the enlightenment can be traced back.

Writing 7th Grade

2.5 Write summaries of reading material including (a) main idea and significant details; (b) use students' words except for quotations; (c) reflect underlying meaning, not just superficial details.

English Language Development

Identify and explain the main ideas and critical details of informational materials, literary text, and text in content areas.

1. Textbook/Assignment Title:_____

2. Chapter/Selection Title: _____

3. Lesson/Article Title:_____

4. Focus: Paraphrase a focus question on the title page, and then write a statement explaining what you will need to be carefully looking for as you read the chapter.

   a. Write a focus question for the first page:_____
   b. Paraphrase the focus question: _____
   c. What I will be looking for: _____

5. Main Idea: Paraphrase the main idea on the title page, then, in your own words, tell you about what the chapter will mainly cover?

   a. Write the main idea on the first page: _____

   b. Tell what the chapter will mainly cover?_____

6. The First Paragraph: Copy the sentence from the first paragraph that best conveys the main idea, that is what the chapter will present about the subject.

   a. The sentence that best states the main idea: _____

7. List three visual aids included in the lesson and describe the concepts, events or processes they will help you understand.

   a. First Visual Aid:_____

b. Concept, event or process it will help you understand: _____

c. Second Visual Aid: _____

d. Concept, event or process it will help you understand: _____

e. Third Visual Aid: _____

f. Concept, event or process it will help you understand: _____

8. Write the first subheadings for Lesson One.

a. First Subheading: _____

b. Write the review question at the end of the first subsection in the lesson: _____

9. Write the second subheadings for Lesson One.

a. Second Subheading: _____

b. Write the review question at the end of the second subsection in the lesson: _

10. Does the lesson have a summary or review at the end of the lesson? _____

a. Read and remember the facts and write the question asked to help you check for understanding:

b. Read and recall the main idea and write a question that will help you remember the main idea.

11. Is there a vocabulary list at the beginning of the chapter?_____

12. List three new terms from the list of key terms, then scan the chapter to find the page on which each is discussed.

First Word:	_____	Page: _____
Second Word:	_____	Page: _____
Third Word:	_____	Page: _____

13. Are there questions included at the beginning of the chapter or in the margins to focus your reading on the main idea?

a. If so, where are they located? _____

b. Write two or more focus questions to help remember the material. _____

To illustrate the concept of keeping students engaged and using context further, reading and writing expository, or narratives, will be explored. By using and teaching expository and narrative material in context, students learn the similarities and differences, as well as how to apply the appropriate strategies and applications to accomplish a specific reading or writing task. Below are two examples that further exemplify this point.

FIGURE 5.6 EXPOSITORY READING

How the Migrant Farm Workers Lived

During the 1960's the migrant worker's lives in the United States were very difficult. Most of the farm workers were Filipinos, Mexican, and African-Americans. Many of these migrant workers were recruited by farm-labor contractors to work on the farms. At that time, the migrant farm workers earned less than $1.20 an hour, plus 20 cents per box of fruit or vegetables they picked. Most of the workers worked less than 120 days per year, while the crops were in season. As a result, these workers barely made enough to pay rent and buy food and cloths for their families. It was difficult for these families to enroll their children into school because they moved frequently to follow the harvesting of the crops. Furthermore, the farmers had no insurance, no paid vacations, holidays, or overtime. Many lived in labor camps that were not fit for human life...

Expository Text-Writing that Informs	Expository Elements-Valuable background information needed to understand characters or actions
Paragraphs	Definition
Essays	Description
Textbook chapters	Time sequence
Editorials	Problem-solving
Articles	Comparison
Reports	Contrast
Manuals	Cause-effect
	Listing
	Process
	Categorization

EXAMPLE STANDARDS

Directions: After reading the above article, fill in the matrix below with background information that the students have identified.

Language Arts/Reading 6th Grade

1.4 Monitor expository text for unknown words with novel meanings by using word, sentence, and paragraph clues to determine meaning.

1.2 Writing Create multiple-paragraph expository compositions.

English Language Development 6th-8th Grades

Reading: Read increasingly complex expository texts aloud with appropriate pacing, intonation and expression.

Writing: Write expository composition (e.g., descriptive, compare, contrast, cause, effect, problem, and solution) that includes a thesis and some points of support.

Rubric (See previous rubric development pp. 28-32).

Point Value or Grade	Problem Solving	Comparison	Contrast	Cause-Effect	Time Sequencing

This is a quick way to assess what the students have understood in relationship to academic objectives, as well as identify areas that need remediation. In addition, over time, patterns for particular students or classrooms can be detected and addressed.

Whereas the above example focused on expository text, the next example focuses on a narrative theme. A rubric such as the one previously used can be utilized to measure meaningful learning in context. However, a single sentence strategy will be introduced to show a different type of assessment for contextual learning.

FIGURE 5.7 NARRATIVE READING

The Early Life of Ritchie Cunningham

Ritchie Cunningham, an Irish American, was born in Boston Massachusetts in 1930. His family owned a boat, which they lost in 1940 when the bank would not renew their loan. From then on, Ritchie and his family became migrant farm workers. They were called migrants because they traveled from one part of the country to another, following the different crops as they became ripe for picking. They picked apples, watermelon, and various nuts on farms so they were also called farm workers.

At 12, Ritchie quit school to become a migrant farm worker to help support his family. In 1950, he was drafted into the Army. In the fall of 1954, Mr. Cunningham married his high school sweetheart, Donna Reed. They had 13 children, and work together on their own farm…

Narrative Text-Writing that tells a story	Narrative Elements
Children's picture books	Setting
Fairy tales	Characters
Short stories	Problems
Novels	Attempts to resolve problems
Fables	Resolution
Myths	Theme or moral
Legends	
Anecdotes	

EXAMPLE STANDARDS

Directions: After students have read the expository text, have them create one sentence that answers the question of who, what, where, when, why, or how.

Language Arts/Listening and Speaking 3rd /4th Grades

2.1 Make brief narrative presentation; provide a context for an incident that is the subject of the presentation, provide insight into why the selected incident is memorable, include well chosen details to develop character, plot, and setting.

2.1 **Writing:** Write narratives: relate ideas, observations, or recollections of an event or experience, provide a context to enable reader to imagine the world of the event or experience, use concrete sensory details, provide insight into why the selected event or experience is memorable.

Rubric

The who, what, where, when, why, and how sentence needs to be written with proper capitalization, be grammatically correct and factual. This is an appropriate way to measure learning in context, and helps students summarize and organize their learning for future recall. Sentences should be grammatically correct, and accurate. This is an excellent example (writing the sentence) of authentic assessment and meaningful learning.

BUILDING CONNECTIONS

An important point to remember is that teachers need to continually build connections and solicit feedback to the materials being taught. This, in turn, increases student learning. It is the dynamics of contextualization that reinforces the attainment of academic standards. Furthermore, context by its Latin root means to weave or tie strings together. In Greek it is used in reference to a carpenter or a builder. Therefore, in the classroom, the teacher, to bring or create a deeper understanding of how all the pieces in a lesson are put together, utilizes contextualization. Without this weaving or building process, nothing is deliberately connected or joined together, resulting in an end product that has a propensity to be haphazard or disjointed. Below is an example of using questions, in context, to create feedback, make connections, and increase a student's ability and motivation to learn

FIGURE 5.8 QUALITY THINKING: MAKING CONNECTIONS

EXAMPLE STANDARDS

Directions: Use the questions listed below as a starting point to solicit feedback and promote quality thinking.

History-Social Science 12th Grade

12.1.1 Analyze the influence of ancient Greek, Roman, English, and leading European political thinkers such as John Locke, Charles-Louis Montesquieu, Niccolo Machiavelli, and William Blackstone on the development of American government.

Visual and Performing Arts Standard 6th Grade

5.4 Describe tactics employed in advertising to sway the viewer's thinking and provide examples.

Knowledge-Identification and recall of information
Who, what, when, where, how _____
Describe _____
Comprehension-Organization and selection of facts and ideas
Retell in your own words. What is the main idea of _____
Application-Use of facts, rules, principles
How is _____ an example of _____
How is _____ related to _____
Why is this significant? _____
Analysis-Separation of a whole into component parts
What are the parts or features of _____
Classify according to outline/diagram/web
How does compare/contrast with _____
What evidence can you present for _____
Synthesis-Combination of ideas to form a new whole _____
What would you predict/infer from_____
What ideas can you add to _____
How would you create/design a new _____
What might happen if you combined with _____

What solutions would you suggest for _____
Evaluation-Development of opinions, judgments, or decisions
Do you agree with_____
What do you think about _____
What is the most important _____
Prioritize according to _____
How would you decide about _____

Creating a contextualized environment can at times seem similar to socialization and collaboration strategies. Although, they can share similar features, for short periods of time, the ultimate objectives are not the same. During socialization or collaboration, students tend to be interacting with each other attempting to solve problems, or misconceptions, about something that has been taught. The students can unintentionally misdirect each other by doing an assignment incorrectly, or coming to erroneous conclusions. In some cases, students focus on gaining the correct answer instead of understanding the process about what they are doing.

However, through the dynamics of contextualization, teaching in the classroom is centered on students learning in context of where a word, phrase, or principle, is to be used in a specific application. It may or may not contain a hands-on segment or involve group work, but this is not a prerequisite. The purpose of the contextualization process is to bring about individual as well as class consensus to a common ground—with common knowledge on which the students can build on and move forward. Likewise, powerful learning opportunities are created when there is a common context and language for describing shared experiences. With this approach, both teacher and students collaborate together to construct a shared framework of understanding academic concepts.

In this contextualized environment, students have ample opportunities to expand their knowledge in context and not separate from it. The earlier examples with nouns and the sea of green clearly demonstrate why this common ground with common knowledge is so important to student learning, and their overall academic success. Without this common knowledge or shared understanding, the students will not be able to successfully communicate with the teacher, or with each other, concerning the lesson or material being taught (Edwards and Mercer, 1987).

Figure 5.9 further elaborates on the importance of feedback, context, and the ability to use these practices to foster both breath and depth of subject matter. Figure 5.8 used Bloom's taxonomy in a brief fashion, figure 5.9 goes into depth. Example standards have been inserted at each level to further enhance this example. This format specifically allows students to explore the subject matter at a profound level of understanding. This format allows the teacher to continually analyze student responses to facilitate their learning.

FIGURE 5.9 USING BLOOM'S TAXONOMY

Directions: Use the outline format to construct a lesson plan for a unit centered on Bloom's Taxonomy. Describe the comprehensive theme of the lesson, the varied activities for each taxonomy level, and activities/discussions/feedback for the lesson, as well as the methods of student assessment to be used in the evaluation process at the end of the unit.

Major Theme:_____

Opening/Culminating Activities: _____

Knowledge Level Task; retrieving information from long term memory.

Language Arts-Reading 3rd Grade

1.0 Word analysis, fluency, and systematic vocabulary development. Students understand the basic features of reading. They select letter patterns and know how to translate them into spoken language by using phonics, syllabication, and word parts. They apply this knowledge to achieve fluent, oral, and silent reading.

Mathematics-Algebra II 8th-12th Grades

5.0 Students demonstrate knowledge of how real and complex numbers are related both arithmetically and graphically. In particular, they can plot complex numbers as points on a plane.

(a) Terminology

Language Arts-Writing 9th-10th Grades

3.11 Evaluate the aesthetic qualities of style, including the impact of diction and figurative language on tone, mood, and theme, using the terminology of literary criticism.

Mathematics-Algebra and Functions 7th Grade

1.4 Use algebraic terminology (e.g., variable, equation, term, coefficient, inequality, expression, constant) correctly.

Who	What	Why	When	Omit	Where	Which
Choose	Find	How	Define	Label	Show	Spell
List	Match	Name	Relate	Tell	Recall	Select

(b) *Specific Facts or Details*

Language Arts-Writing 7th Grade

1.2 Support all statements and claims with anecdotes, descriptions, facts, and statistics, with specific examples.

English Language Development-Reading 6th-8th Grades

Read and orally identify main ideas and details of informational materials, literary text and text in content area using simple sentences.

- What is_____?
- Where is_____?
- How did _____ happen?
- When did_____ happen?
- Can you recall_____?
- Who was_____?

(c) *Classification and Categories*

Science-Focus on Earth Science 6th Grade

5c Students know populations of organisms can be categorized by the functions they serve in an ecosystem.

Mathematics-Measurement and Geometry 1st Grade

2.0 Classify familiar plane and solid objects by common attributes, such as color, position, shape, size, roundness, or number of corners, and explain which attributes are being used for classification.

- Which one_____?
- How is_____?
- Can you select_____?
- Making a simple grid and having some predetermined headings or letting students create their own is an excellent way to assess how well students can classify or categorize items. Theses types of activities facilitates students develop of organizational, analytical, and recall skills.

Mammals	Reptiles	Same Characteristics	Different Characteristics

(d) Principles and Generalizations

History-Social Science-United States History and Geography: Making a New Nation 5th Grade

5.7.3 Understand the fundamental principles of American constitutional democracy, including how the government derives its power from the people and the primacy of individual liberty.

Mathematics-Mathematical Reasoning 7th Grade

3.3 Develop generalizations of the results obtained and the strategies used and apply them to new problem situations.

- Why did_____?

- When did_____?

- Identify how selected principles of design are used in a work of ___ and how they affect personal responses to and evaluation of the work of _____.

- An example that can be used to assess what general principles students use to solve a specific problem would be to have students list some problems on the left side of a piece of paper and solutions on the right. Then have them match what principle with which solution and why. This is an effective strategy to assess skill attainment and recognition; as well as students' comprehension, in relationship to their developmental level, and ability to transfer and understand.

(e) Theories, Models, and Structures

Language Arts-Reading 4th Grade

3.4 Compare and contrast tales from different cultures by tracing the exploits of one character type and develop theories to account for similar tales in other cultures.

Science-Investigation and Experimentation 9th-12th Grades

1g Recognize the usefulness and limitations of models and theories as scientific representations of reality

- How would you demonstrate_____?

- How would you explain_____?
- Can you list the four....?

(f) *Subject Specific Skills and Techniques*

English Language Development 9th-12th Grades

Identify techniques which have specific rhetorical or aesthetic purposes in literary tests (e.g., irony, tone, mood, sound of language).

Visual and Performing Arts-Visual Arts 7th Grade

5.4 Identify professions in or related to the visual arts and some of the specific skills needed for those professions.

- How would you describe_____?

(g) *Strategic Knowledge Needed*

History-Social Science 10th Grade

10.8.3 Identify and locate the Allied and Axis powers on a map and discuss the major turning points of the war, the principal theaters of conflict, key strategic decisions, and the resulting war conferences and political resolutions, with emphasis on the importance of geographical factors.

- Who were the main_____?
- Which one_____?

(h) *Contextual and Conditional Knowledge needed to perform cognitive task*

Language Arts-Reading 7th Grade

1.0 Word analysis, fluency, and systematic vocabulary development. Students use their knowledge of word origins and word relationships, as well as historical and literary context clues, to determine the meaning of specialized vocabulary and to understand the precise meaning of grade-level appropriate words.

Comprehension Level Task; understanding the meaning of oral, written, and graphic instructional messages.

Language Arts-Reading 8th Grade

2.0 Reading comprehension with a focus on informational materials. Students read and understand grade level appropriate material. They describe and connect the essential ideas, arguments, and perspectives of the text by using their knowledge of text structure, organization, and purpose.

(a) Interpret

Language Arts-Reading 4th Grade

1.6 Distinguish and interpret words with multiple meanings.

Mathematics-Algebra and Functions 4th Grade

1.2 Interpret and evaluate mathematical expressions that use parenthesis.

- How would you state or interpret in your own words?
- What is meant by_____?
- How would you summarize_____?

(b) Exemplify

History-Social Science-Continuity and Change 3rd Grade

3.4.3 ...know essential landmarks, symbols, and documents that create a sense of community among citizens and exemplify cherished ideals (e.g., the U.S. flag, the bald eagle, the Statue of Liberty, the U.S. Constitution, the Declaration of Independence, the U.S. Capitol).

- What facts or ideas show_____?
- What is the best answer?

(c) Classify

Science-Focus on Earth Science 6th Grade

6b Students know the different energy and material resources, including air, soil, rocks, minerals, petroleum, fresh water, wildlife, and forest, and know how to classify them as renewable or nonrenewable.

- How would you classify this type of_____?

(d) Summarize

History-Social Science-Historical and Social Science Analysis Skills K-5th Grades

1 Students summarize key events of the era they are studying and explain the historical contexts of those events.

- How would you rephrase the meaning?

(e) Infer

Science-Investigation and Experimentation 4th Grade

6a Differentiate observation from inference (interpretation) and know scientists' explanations come partly from what they observe and partly from how they interpret their observations.

- What can you say about_____?
- Locate instances of unsupported inferences, fallacious reasoning, and propaganda in text.

(f) Compare

Mathematics-Statistics, Data Analysis, and Data Probability 5th Grade

1.0 Students display, analysis, compare, and interpret different data sets, including data sets of different sizes.

- How would you compare_____?
- The students ability to comparing and contrasting can be assessed by giving them a prompt and having them answer the question from both sides of the issue. It is a good technique to identify barriers to learning. It also serves as a catalyst for identifying values, biases, and gaps in knowledge or information.

(g) Explain

Science-Focus on Physical Science 8th Grade

5d Students know the idea of atoms explains the conservation of matter; In chemical reactions, the number of atoms stays the same no matter how they are arranged, so that the total mass stays the same.

- Which statements support_____?
- Can you explain_____?

Compare	Contrast	Demonstrate	Interpret	Explain
Extend	Illustrate	Infer	Outline	Restate
Rephrase	Translate	Summarize	Show	Classify

Application Level Task; carrying out or using a procedure in a given situation or specific time frame.

Mathematics-Calculus 8th-12th Grades

27.0 Students know the techniques of solution of selected elementary differential equations and their applications to a wide variety of situations, including growth-and decay problems.

(a) *Executing*

Visual and Performing Arts-Dance 6th Grade

1.3 Identify and use force/energy variations when executing...

- What approach would you use to_____?
- How would you apply what you have learned to develop_____?
- How would you solve_____ using what you have learned?
- Can you make use of the fact to_____?
- What facts would you choose to show_____?
- An activity to use application in the classroom is to give the students an authentic prompt on a topic that they are familiar with. Along with some excerpts on the topic, have students write a response. They need to determine who the response is being directed to and what their role in writing the response. This activity hones students analytical and application skills specific to their developmental level.

(b) *Implementing*

History-Social Science-United States History and Geography: Growth and Conflict 8th Grade

8.2.2 Analyze the Articles of Confederation and the Constitution and the success of each in implementing the ideals of the Declaration of Independence.

- How would you show your understanding of_____?
- How would you use_____?
- What examples can you find to_____?
- What other way would you plan to_____?
- What elements would you choose to change_____?
- What questions would you ask in an interview and with whom_____?

Apply	Build	Choose
Construct	Develop	Interview
Make use of	Organize	Experiment with
Plan	Select	Solve
Utilize	Model	Identify

Analysis Level Task; breaking material into its various components and determining how each component functions in relationship to other parts and to the overall structure or purpose.

Mathematics-Measurement and Geometry 7th Grade

1.3 Use measures expressed as rates (e.g., speed, density) and measures expressed as products (e.g., person-days) to solve problems; check the units of the solutions; and use dimensional analysis to check the reasonableness of the answer.

(a) Differentiate

Mathematics-Measurement and Geometry 5th Grade

1.4 Differentiate between, and use appropriate units of measures for, two-and three-dimensional objects (i.e., find the perimeter, area, volume).

Language Arts-Listening and Speaking 8th Grade

2.4b Differentiate fact from opinion and support argument with detailed evidence, examples, and reasoning.

- What are the parts or features of_____?
- What do you think?
- Can you list the parts of_____?
- What inferences can you make?
- Can you identify the different parts?
- What is the relationship between_____?
- Can you make a difference between_____?

(b) Organize

Language Arts-Writing 6th Grade

1.3 Use a variety of effective coherent organizational patterns, including comparison and contrast; organization by categories; and arrangement by spatial notes, order of importance, or climatic order.

- How is x related to y?
- What is the theme?
- How would you classify x or y?
- How would you categorize?

- One way to analyze how well students are making connections to the material is through a webbing activity. This can be done by having students write a concept in the middle of a piece of paper. Have them draw lines to other concepts or principles that relate to the concept. These drawings produce a web that indicates how students organize and relate parallel concepts to each other. This exercise can also be used as a prewriting activity for planning a report or essay.

(c) Attribute

Mathematics-Measurement and Geometry 3rd Grade

2.0 Students describe and compare attributes of plane and solid geometric figures and use their understanding to show relationships and solve problems.

- What motive is there?
- What conclusions can you draw?
- What is the function of_____?
- What evidence can you find?
- What ideas justify_____?

Analyze	Relationships	Test for	Examine
Compare	Inference	Distinction	Survey
Dissect	Categorize	Function	Theme
Inspect	Contrast	Assumption	Distinguish
Take part in	Divide	Classify	Motive
List	Simplify	Discover	Conclusion

Synthesis Level Task; creating and putting elements together to form a new coherent whole or form an original product.

History-Social Science-World History and Geography: Medieval and Early Modern Times 7th Grade

7.6.8 Understand the importance of the Catholic Church as apolitical, intellectual, and aesthetic institution (e.g., founding of universities, political and spiritual roles of the clergy, creation of monastic and mendicant religious orders, preservation of the Latin language and religious texts, St. Thomas Aquinas's synthesis of classical philosophy with Christian theology and the concept of natural law.

(a) Generate

Language Arts-Reading 9th/10th Grades

2.3 Generate relevant questions about readings on issues that can be researched.

- What would happen if_____?
- Can you elaborate on the reason?
- How would you adapt x to create a different y?
- What way would you design_____?
- Suppose you could x what would you do?
- Can you formulate a theory for_____?
- Can you think of an original way for the_____?

Build	Minimize	Solution	Imagine
Compile	Theorize	Modify	Originate
Create	Improve	Improve	Propose
Estimate	Choose	Maximize	Suppose
Invent	Compose	Elaborate	Change
Plan	Design	Happen	Adapt
Solve	Formulate	Combine	Delete
Discuss	Make up	Construct	Test
Original	Predict	Develop	Change

What changes would you make to solve_____?

- Can you propose an alternative?
- How could you change or modify the plot or plan?
- How would you test?
- Can you predict the outcome if_____?

(b) Produce

Visual and Performing Arts-Theater-9th-12th Grades

2.3 Design, produce, or perform scenes or plays from a variety of theatrical periods and styles…

- How would you improve_____?

- Can you invent_____?

- What could be done to maximize_____?

- What could be done to minimize_____?

- What could be combined to improve or change_____?

- How would you estimate the results for_____?

- What facts can you compile_____?

- Can you construct a model that would change_____?

- Getting students to recognize problems instead of just getting the answer is an important aspect of a student's development. Students need to know how to make adequate connections to solve problems in a variety of ways. A way this can be accomplished is to write down three or four different scenarios and have students identify what they think the problem is, as well as list some plausible solutions. As students learn to apply information to increasingly complex tasks, they develop their individual active learning strategies.

Evaluation Level Task; making judgments based on criteria and academic standards.

Language Arts-Reading 5th Grade

3.6 Evaluate the meaning of archetypal patterns and symbols that are found in myth and tradition by using literature from different eras and cultures.

(a) Check

Mathematics-Mathematical Reasoning 6th Grade

2.7 Make precise calculations and check the validity of the results from the context of the problem.

History-Social Science-World History and Geography: Ancient Civilizations 6th Grade

6.7.2 Describe the government of the Roman Republic and its significance (e.g., written constitution and tripartite government, checks and balances, civic duty).

- What would you recommend?

- How would you rate the_____?

- What would you cite to defend the actions?

- Can you assess the value or importance of_____?

- How could you determine_____?

- What would you select?

- How would you prioritize?

- What information would you use to support the view?

- Why was it better that_____?

- How would you prioritize the facts?

- Students need to become good problem solvers. One activity to assess, not only how to solve problems but diagnosing the students' process, is as follows: List a problem on the board or overhead. List all the strategies that the students come up with to solve the problem. Next, try to hone in more specifically on which step should be done first and so on. This activity develops students' critical thinking and problem solving skills. It also is a transferable skill for active learning.

(b) Critique

Language Arts-Reading 11th Grade

2.6 Critique the power, validity, and truthfulness of arguments set forth in public documents; their appeal to both friendly and hostile audiences; and the extent to which arguments anticipate and address reader concerns and counterclaims (e.g., appeal to reason, to authority, to pathos, and emotion).

- Do you agree with the actions?

- Do you agree with the outcome?

- What is your opinion of_____?

- How would you prove_____?

- How would you disprove?

- Would it be better if_____?

- What did they (the character) choose?

- How would you evaluate_____?

- What choice would you make?

- What judgments would you make?

- Based on what information you know, how would you explain_____?

- How would you justify_____?

- What data was used to make connections?

- How would you compare the ideas?

Award	Prove	Appraise	Measure
Criticize	Influence	Interpret	Rate
Determine	Estimate	Importance	Select
Judge	Choose	Disprove	Prioritize
Compare	Decide	Perceive	Explain
Recommend	Dispute	Influence	Criteria
Agree	Justify	Conclude	Assess
Opinion	Mark	Defend	Value
Support	Rule on	Evaluate	Deduct

Fluency/Flexibility Level Task:

Originality/Elaboration Level Task:

Risk-Taking/Complexity Level Task:

Curiosity/Imagination Level Task:

Methods Of Student Assessment/Rubric:_____

(Adapted from Anderson, et al, 2001).

SHIFTING THE FOCUS

Anderson (2002), states that the curricular focus of student responsive classrooms requires a shift from what students know and can do to what they know and can do as a result of what they are learning. Contextualization supports this shift, in part because it is a broader construct about student learning. It takes into account previously acquired knowledge, learned partially or improperly, and identifies how these can produce barriers for learning. Overcoming these barriers with new material, applied in the present, in context, produces new meaningful learning, which is understood by the student. In practical terms, the students understand what they have learned (e.g., nouns), and know when they see a noun (e.g., Washington D.C.) they can identify it as such.

CONTEXTUALIZATION AND MEANINGFUL LEARNING

Meaningful learning takes place when students can apply subject matter learned to authentic situations. In other words, when students can create meaning from classroom instruction, whether it is oral, written, graphic, or text, and apply this information correctly, academic understanding has taken place. This is an important concept because the quicker a student can grasp a concept, the more they stay on task, hence, the more they learn.

FIGURE ACTIVITY 5.10 MEANINGFUL LEARNING LESSON PLAN

EXAMPLE STANDARDS

Directions: Use the outline to create a meaningful learning activity. Choose a problem that requires multiple steps or has multiple aspects. See how well the students are listening by receiving feedback at each step of the lesson. Record the primary purpose of the academic assignment, the decisions to be made when designing the task, and the process for determining the assessment when the activity is completed.

Language Arts 11th Grade

3.5c Evaluate the philosophical, political, religious, ethical, and social influences of the historical period that shaped the characters, plots, and settings.

History-Social Science 4th Grade

4.2/4.3 Students describe and explain the social, political, cultural, and economic life and interactions among early people of California until statehood.

Visual and Performing Arts

3.1 Examine and describe or report on the role of a work of art created to make a social comment or protest social conditions.

Purpose: _____

Decisions to be made: _____

Time frames:_____

Resources to be used: _____

Role/responsibility: _____

Social skills to be emphasized (if applicable): _____

Academic standard to be emphasized: _____

Behavioral skills to be emphasized (if applicable): _____

Individual accountability (if applicable): _____

Project/task accountability: _____

Another method to assess what has been hard to understand, unclear, or something that is confusing, is to have students write down any questions, comments, or concerns. These are then turned into the teacher at the end of a topic, theme, or other specific period of time. Because context and application is a dynamic process involving information and its immediate use, some students will find certain aspects of the lesson difficult to grasp or learn. Using this practice allows the teacher to review what students are not sure about through their own personal viewpoints. The teacher can then utilize this feedback, to make future adjustments, to better facilitate student learning. Over time, students will develop the ability to articulate questioning strategies that will aid them in their development of personal active learning strategies.

In summary, contextualization is the interplay between the teacher, content, and the students. It is putting the materials and academic standards into perspectives that the students comprehend. In this environment, students are able to express their perceptions and to challenge what they do not understand. The more that is taught in the classroom through context the quicker students can learn and create new strategies of problem solving. Contextualization demystifies academic language, concepts, and principles for the students. This is an essential necessity for second language learners because they are not familiar with English sentence structures, or obscure words like spool, cable, crew, wired, etc. Just as academic standards must be taught with high expectations, so contextualization strategies need to be utilized so students can gain mastery and demonstrate academic competence. Without this component, the students can be victimized not for what they don't know, but what they can not express in language, sentence structure, or vocabulary. Without context the weaver has an endless string that continually tangles, and the carpenter, with all the materials needed, never gets to complete the task.

POSITIVE PRAISE

Contextualization builds on a foundation of positive feedback. Through positive feedback, the teacher encourages the students. Because the interactions are continuous and immediate, the teacher validates the students by demonstrating that they are willing to help them. This fosters a comfort level with the students because the teacher is actively giving their time, energy, and expertise to optimize the students' academic growth. As students experience and acknowledge the teachers' efforts, they tend to be more attentive, put out more effort, and have a higher level of interest to learn.

Through the use of positive praise and timely feedback, the teacher emphasizes skills that contribute to the students' motivation. These include:

- Explaining to their students the reality that most perform better in one subject area but not necessarily in all areas, everyone has strengths and weaknesses;

- Demonstrating how to set realistic timelines to get task done,

- Teaching and monitoring a repertoire of effective strategies to be utilized to complete assignments,

- Self-monitor through the use of rubrics and posted work to guide and appraise progress towards completion of tasks, and

- Make adjustments as needed (Zimmerman, 1989).

As active participants in their own learning, students have better opportunities to reconstruct previous learned principles to new experiences and circumstances. The students are encouraged to look beyond the answer to understand the process of why a certain response is correct.

In addition, because of their positive classroom ambiance, students feel secure and want to learn, and therefore they do (Pianta, 1995). The students, because of the teacher's use of active teaching strategies have internalized a belief that school is not just an institution surrounded by four walls. Instead, they believe they are the seeds for the future. They know they are unique individuals and are treated as such. Because of the way the teacher has interacted with them, the students know they are valid individuals with thoughts and feelings associated with their school experience (Piaget, 1981). This is of paramount importance because these perceptions are the catalyst for how the students think, learn, and act. The students know they can be expressive and this helps to motivate them to take greater risk. Assignments are task specific so they have ample opportunities to gain mastery as well as receive immediate and meaningful feedback on their academic endeavors. Research has shown that students are more conducive to learning when it occurs in a positive classroom, one encouraging interaction, trust, and order (McCombs and Whisler, 1997).

Students desire teachers to instruct them in positive ways that acknowledges them as individuals. In classrooms where there is positive praise and feedback, all students, including those considered at-risk, out performed their peers. (Daniels, and Kalkman, 2001).

STUDENT REFINEMENT AND IMPROVEMENT

Teachers continually challenge students to find satisfaction in their completed assignments and their personal sense of accomplishment. This helps students acquire information in a way that builds on who they are and compliments their various learning styles. Likewise, this process guides students to become more responsible and take ownership over their own learning (Mitra, 2002). Students are not co-dependents of the teachers, but motivated from internal forces they have control over. There is a philosophical shift from what the teacher is teaching to value what the student is learning. The more students learn, the more a teacher challenges them to greater heights. Teachers continually encourage students to assume more responsibility as they prod them forward (Hogan and Tudge, 1999). Empowerment is further enhanced by teachers giving students ample opportunities to use information learned to solve similar problems. This gives the students practice so they can perfect their problem solving skills; and allows them the opportunity to teach these same skills to each other (Webb, Troper, and Fall 1995).

When teachers demonstrate to students that they deserve and expect answers to their questions, Nelson-Le Gall and Resnick (1998), findings indicate the students experience a personal sense of empowerment. In this light, students need to continually articulate their ideas about strategy usage and assignment criteria that are meaningful to them. Elder and Paul's (2001) research on critical thinking demonstrates these empowering principles in practice. As students employ these strategies, with both their teacher and peers, they are further empowered, and experience a deeper sense of accomplishment.

FIGURE 5.11 UNIVERSAL INTELLECTUAL STANDARDS

EXAMPLE STANDARDS

Listening and Speaking 10th Grade.

1.12 Evaluate the clarity, quality, effectiveness, and general coherence of a speaker's important points, arguments, evidence, organization of ideas, delivery, diction, and syntax.

English Language Development.

Analyze how clarity is affected by patterns of organization, hierarchical structures, repetition of key ideas, syntax, and word choice in text across context areas.

Directions: Encourage students to use these intellectual standards to better communicate their points of view.

Clarity

- Could you elaborate on that point further?
- Can that point be expresses in a different way?
- Could you give an illustration?
- Could you give an example?

Accuracy

- Is that really true?
- How could we check that?

Precision

- Could you give me more details?
- Could you be more specific?

Relevance

- How is that connected to the question?
- How does that bear on the issue?

Depth

- How does your answer address the complexities in the question?
- How are you taking into account the problems in the question?
- Is that dealing with the most significant factors?

Breadth

- Do we need to consider another point of view?
- Is there another way to look at that question?
- What would this look like from a conservative/liberal point of view?
- What would this look like from the point of view of...

Logic

- Does this really make sense?
- Does the following mean what you said?
- How does that follow?
- Before you implied this and now you are saying that-are both positions true?

These intellectual standards are another tool to help facilitate context, empowerment, and student understanding. This also is an effective method to get the students to articulate the 'what and why' of their thinking and learning. This occurs by them using a common language understood by all.

CONCLUSION

Active teaching is based on the premise that a student responsive pedagogy is one where the students learn how to learn and succeed in the classroom. Lewis' (2003) research demonstrated that instructional practices should contain certain beliefs about students. These include:

- That students will achieve when they are effectively taught how to learn because achievement is not innately determined.
- An educator's responsibility is to discover and build upon students strengths.

- Schools cannot blame students, families, or poverty for underachievement; instructional strategies need to be evaluated.

- Each individual staff member must examine his or her beliefs and change practices [if necessary]…

- Schools should be considered excellent only when all students are achieving at high levels (Lewis, 2003).

Teachers, as demonstrated by the above characteristics of active teaching, are, reflective of their practice, as well as proactive in their pedagogy. They foster and develop warm and trusting relationships with their students. They know they have a real impact on their lives. By using student responsive instructional practices, that are data driven, teachers can help students set and achieve goals that are realistic, specific, and attainable, helping all their students succeed.

When active teaching is successful, students understand academic information and the associated task outcomes. They are able to discuss the standards learned with confidence, as well as describe the strategies used to gain mastery. Rather than always provide direct instruction on predefined strategies, teachers collaborate with students to define and articulate strategy choice. Likewise, all strategies are taught over time and in depth so students have many opportunities to understand, maintain, and generalize what they have learned. In this manner, the students have acquired a wide array of strategies to be utilized and adapted. This creates a cycle that promotes cognitive activities like task analysis, differentiated strategy selection, and other self monitoring skills.

The following chapter will illustrate what the students need to do as a result of being in classrooms where active teaching occurred daily.

CHAPTER 6

ACTIVE LEARNING: WHAT STUDENTS DO

Students will never do well if they do not try. Lack of effort can occur as a result of negative perceptions, attitudes, poor motivation, insufficient commitment, and lack of understanding. In many classrooms, the purpose of academic task and activities are not fully understood by students, regardless of the quality of the lesson delivered (Perkins, 1985). In actuality, many students in school do not think as skillfully or critically as teachers would like or expect. Therefore, students need to develop active learning strategies to understand and fulfill the academic requirements of any assignment.

Without the skills associated with active learning, students will not have a repertoire of strategies to be able to make the necessary adjustments to complete assignments successfully. Regrettably, many students are ineffective learners simply because they have not been guided in proper questioning or strategy use. That is, they do not know what they are not sure of. Because of this, the students do not know how to communicate or articulate their needs effectively to the teacher.

When students fail to engage in the dynamics of active learning, they resist adapting and modifying their strategies even when they know these strategies are ineffective, too time consuming, or are applicable in a much narrower application. Narrower applications can include; using addition instead of multiplication, creative spelling instead of learning how to spell words correctly, and using a limited amount of reading strategies regardless of the purpose (Lester, 1994; Pressley and Afflerbach, 1995). The end result of this cycle of failure is students, who are frustrated, and lack the confidence, or ability, within themselves to succeed.

ACTIVE LEARNERS: INTERNALIZING PROCESSES FOR SUCCESS

According to Kiewra (2002), explicit strategy instruction is rarely taught or incorporated into lesson plans or the curriculum. Students can be taught how to be active participants through embedded strategy instruction. This is a short term method, taught by the teacher, within a lesson or academic task. The process is two-fold. The

Rock and Michelle Moore MiRoc Publishing @ AOL.Com

first is to get the students to master an academic standard or task. The second is to learn suggested strategies which help facilitate the acquisition of new learning principles. These active learning methods include the following embedded strategies:

FIGURE 6.1 INFUSING STRATEGIES INTO INSTRUCTION

- Time Management
  - Time Lines
  - Benchmarks/Check points
  - Due date postings
  - Time Rubrics
- Organization Skills
  - Strategies that organize or facilitate recall
  - Use period/subject agendas to make sure students know a day or week's event.
  - Journal how school day/homework is divided and used.
- Research Methods
- Note Taking (i.e., T-notes, Cornell)
  - Outlines by students themselves
  - Class notes or partial outlines supplied by teacher
  - Teacher can provide students with outlines that are in a cloze format, complete outlines that can be used as a study guide, or a partial outline that students have to complete various portions during classroom discussions. Webbing activities can also be used as a note taking strategy. All classroom outlines need to have a specific focus so that students learn the process. This will facilitate the students' internalization of these techniques.
- Various Text Learning Strategies
  - Pre-reading
  - Narrative
  - Expository
  - Reading for specific purpose, etc.
  - Critical thinking can be prompted by teaching students how to analyze literature pieces to look at specific aspects like intent or content. This method

allows students to discover how they can find common patterns or structures within various genres, etc.

- Other application strategies
  - Writing
  - Math
  - Scientific Reasoning
- Studying
  - Able to explain reasoning for an answer
  - Monitor choice selections
  - A practice for decision-making or having to look at more than one aspect of a problem can be done by having students list opposite or alternative ideas in columns on a piece of paper. This strategy promotes critical thinking because all choices have consequences.
- Test taking techniques.

SHORT TERM SUPPORTS

Embedded strategy instruction is helpful when exposing students to different problem solving methods. However, students need to move away from any dependency on the teacher as the sole provider of strategy choice. It needs to be mentioned that active learners are self-regulated, and self-efficacious, not co-dependents of the teacher. These students need to evolve in their learning to effectively implement task specific strategies to facilitate the attainment and mastery of academic standards. This is important because through this dynamic process the students learn to trust in their abilities. It is important to note that strategy instruction—directed by the teacher to the student—is not an efficient practice to produce self-sufficient learners. The emphasis in the classroom should never be explicitly on teachers instructing students on how to use predefined strategies. This method may help students arrive at an answer or complete an objective, but it can also inadvertently exclude the student from internalizing their own problem-solving processes. Instead, what's required is focused attention on how students adapt their strategies to the various tasks. The teacher, along with the students, need to collaborate together to find the best strategies that will work for the task at hand. This is not to say that the teacher should not anticipate potential problems and know what strategies will probably be the most useful for students. But to promote optimal strategy implementation, requires the students' active participation. This entails the use of previously learned strategies, and the evaluation on why those specific strategies did or did not work. The students need to articulate clearly why they need to revise or modify strategies. This revision is based on new insight and information gleamed from the completed assignment. Thus, the students know within themselves the why and how of the strategy choice, a foundational component of active learning

COGNITIVE CYCLES

Other ways that students can learn to be active participants in their strategy development are through the ability to:

- **Self acquire the ability to set goals,**

- **Evaluate and reflect on academic task, and**

- **Utilize various techniques gleamed from classroom instruction, and through social, cognitive, and contextual interactions, that occur in the classroom.**

While trying to build self-sustaining strategies, students need to internalize practices that are more effective. They need to understand and use posted rubrics, analyze key information in anchor assignments, and create other helps that will facilitate their personal success.

Active or self-regulated learning is not about students possessing superior mental capabilities or keenly developed academic skills. It is a self-directive process where students cognitively focus on accomplishing specific academic goals. Students who are active learners tend to practice self-regulated plans of action and possess high levels of self-efficacy. As such, these learners are generally defined as students who are "meta-cognitively, motivationally, and behaviorally active participants in their own learning process" (Zimmerman, 1989, p. 329).

Active learners do not possess special innate characteristics; nor are the students' anomalies. Their perceived peculiarity is due in part, because they have learned how to be self-sufficient. They are continuously engaging in a cycle of cognitive activities, which gives them the ability to work through their academic tasks (Butler, and Winne, 1995). The students, as active learners, have established within themselves deliberate plans of action to accomplish specific academic tasks. These include: setting specific short term goals, using appropriate strategies for attainment of objectives, self-monitoring of progress, effective time management, and a disposition to continually learn new techniques to solve problems (Martinez-Pons, 1996, Zimmermann, Bonner, and Kovach, 1996). As a result, the students are in the process of becoming independent learners.

SELF-EFFICACY

"Efficacy beliefs influence how people [students] think, feel, motivate themselves, and act" (Bandura, 1994, p. 7). It is a mind set that students possess. They trust in their personal capacity to learn and master academic standards. These students have a positive self-perception about their competence, and ability to succeed in the goals they set for themselves. Positive beliefs connect academic outcomes to controllable factors like the application of effort to work accomplished, or the use of differentiated strategies for different tasks. This competence fosters a student's capacity to succeed, and leads directly to motivation. Thus, students develop the conviction that they have some control over their lives.

FIGURE 6.2 ONE DOZEN ACTIVE LEARNING PRACTICES

The following characteristics have been found to be successful practices for active learners. These principals form the foundation for active learners.

- They understand and can analyze task demands to determine what is required. The students understand the overall assignment. They see the big picture.

- The students have examined the outcome procedures such as grading criteria, process, procedure, research, organization, presentation, and referencing. They understand the various portions of an assignment, and know what is expected for each.

- Task analysis—the students know what strategies need to be used and why. Their repertoire of different strategies has been internalized so that they can vary choice at will. This cuts time and builds their confidence.

- The students believe that they can do the assignments. These perceptions are based on previous strategy usage and the success from past assignments.

- The students know how to monitor their progress and make adjustments accordingly. They have mastered the art of time management.

- Lastly, the students solicit feedback from others to diagnose potential problems and to find solutions to complete their academic task.

ACTIVE LEARNER STRATEGIES

Students can further hone their skills when preparing for a test or acquiring classroom information by internalizing techniques through their meta-cognitive strategy development. Activities contained in the following figures facilitate student confidence and self-efficacy. Some examples are variations of previously used active teaching strategies with a different emphasis or application. Others have subtle variations which change their purpose completely. This list is by no way exhaustive, but is meant to serve as a starting point to sensitize one to the realm of active learning. These strategies, once internalized by the students, help them become more self-reflective, active, and independent learners. In addition, these skills can be transferred to other learning situations that occur throughout the students' school day.

FIGURE 6.3 STUDYING FOR A TEST

EXAMPLE STANDARDS

Language Arts-Reading 1st Grade

2.2 Respond to who what, where, when, how questions.

Writing 9th Grade

2.4 Students structure ideas and arguments in a sustained and logical fashion. Use specific rhetorical devices to support assertions. Clarify and defend positions with precise and relevant evidence, including facts, expert opinion, and logical reasoning.

Visual and Performing Arts 7th-9th Grades

4.2 Identify and apply criteria-based assessments for personal use.

Identify the information to be covered on the test.

- **Active Learning Implications:** When students prepare for tests, they can use various techniques to direct and guide review of the material.

- **Goal:** From the above three example standards, students need to:

    1. Identify and recall specific events with 5 W's and 1 H using external study aids.

    2. Structure ideas in a systematic and logical format.

    3. Understand specific criteria and learn for the assessment.

- **Active Learners Responsibility:** To be responsible and develop basic study aids to help retain information on any given topic.

- **Student Responsive Design in Practice**

    Academics: Students need to know the standards the assignment is based on. This helps establish purpose and reason for academic mastery. Students also need to understand the assessment criteria and the due date. This will help focus their efforts to complete the task correctly and in a timely manner.

    Social/Collaborative: Students can develop study groups to go over the who, what where, when, why, and how, practice oral assignment in front of others, and receive constructive feedback.

    Contextual: Students can tie assignment into the context of the time, lesson, etc. to reinforce their learning. Context facilitates the use of logic.

Cognitive/Developmental: Students need to ask themselves; do I need more background information, key vocabulary, or use a different strategy to learn material effectively? Is my layout of the information logical?

Other suggestions on how this can be accomplished:

Identify and collect all necessary materials (e.g., textbook, notebook, etc.).

Understand grading criteria clearly.

Identify major topics.

Under each topic identify major headings.

Under each heading identify Who, What, Where, When, How, and Why.

Write this information on the outline form (figure 6.4) or underline/highlight it.

Make study aids such as flash cards.

Create a matrix to list sequential events.

Flash Card Study Aid to help review for test or assess knowledge learned.

Questions

Topic:

Who:

What:

Where:

When:

How

Why:

FIGURE 6.4 STUDENT GENERATED OUTLINES

EXAMPLE STANDARDS

Reading 6th Grade

2.4 Clarify an understanding of texts by creating outlines, logical notes, and summaries.

History-Social Science 8th Grade

8.6.2 Outline the physical obstacles to the economic and political factors involved in building a network of roads, canals, and railroads.

Science 9th Grade

1d. Students know the central dogma of molecular biology outlines the flow of information from transcription of ribonucleic acid in the nucleus to translation of proteins on ribosome in the cytoplasm.

- **Active Learning Implications:** Students use outlines to organize information or study for a test. They practice writing questions from the outline form and then answer them. If study questions are provided, they answer all questions. Purpose is to make certain that all information in the outline is thoroughly understood.

- **Goal:** From the above three example standards, students need to:

  1. Create outlines, notes, summaries, and diagrams.

  2. Identify economic and political barriers through outlines.

  3. Outline a sequence of events.

- **Active Learners Responsibility:** To be responsible and self motivated and to learn how to organize basic information about any topic through outlines and summaries.

- **Student Responsive Design in Practice**

  Academics: Students need to know the standards the assignment is based on. This helps establish purpose and reason for academic mastery. Students also need to understand the assessment criteria and the due date. This will help focus their efforts to complete the task correctly and in a timely manner.

  Social/Collaborative: Students can develop study groups to go over outlines, summaries, notes or diagrams together. They could also assign each in their group a portion to be learned. It will be the individual's responsibility to share information to others in the study group. Students should know materials well enough to critique each other as to the accuracy of information.

  Contextual: Students can tie diagrams into the pattern of which it occurs. Students can write notes and put them in the order of events to reinforce learning.

  Cognitive/Developmental: Students need to ask themselves; do I need more background information, key vocabulary, or use a different strategy to learn material effectively? Do I really understand what I wrote on my notes? Is this outline helping me? Is their anything missing?

Suggestions on how this can be accomplished:

  Double column notes divided into economic and political factors.

  Create sequential work sheet or time frame checklist to help keep events in order.

  Simple outline format

Subject:

Topic:

General:

Specific:

Who:

What:

Where:

When:

How:

Why:

Vocabulary:
  (McCarney, Wunderlish, Bauer, 1993, pp. 498-499).

FIGURE 6.5 STUDENT GENERATED PRACTICE JOURNALS

EXAMPLE STANDARDS

History-Social Science-Principles of American Democracy and Economics 12th Grade

12.9.1 Explain how the different philosophies and structures of feudalism, mercantilism, socialism, fascism, communism, monarchies, parliamentary, systems, and constitutional liberal democracies influence economic policies, social welfare policies, and human rights practices.

Visual and Performing Arts-Theatre 9th-12th Grades

1.2 Document observations and perceptions…

- **Active Learning Implications**: For students to write down possible applications for a principle (theory, procedure, topic) that was discussed. This method helps students generalize something they have learned and gives them a visual picture of how it can be applied in other contexts. It facilitates reasoning, thinking for oneself, inference, and other critical thinking strategies.

- **Goal:** From the above two example standards students need to:

  1. Explain various philosophies and their influences on several democratic principles.

  2. Document various observations and perceptions.

- **Active Learners Responsibility:** Students need to invest time to understand theories, concepts, and subject matter in depth and be able to apply information to new or adaptive settings. They also need to develop writing skills to reflect and articulate what has been learned in their own words.

- **Student Responsive Design in Practice**
  Academics: Students need to know the standards the assignment is based on. This helps establish purpose and reason for academic mastery. Students also need to understand the assessment criteria and the due date. This will help focus their efforts to complete the task correctly and in a timely manner.

  Social/Collaborative: Students can write in their journals and have others read it. Does the entry make sense? Can another read it and make sense of what was learned by the writer?

  Contextual: What is the context of the journal entry? If you came back in a week or a month from now and re-read the entry, would it still make sense? Could you duplicate the findings that the entry illustrated?

  Cognitive/Developmental: Students need to ask themselves; do I need more background information, key vocabulary, or use a different strategy to learn material effectively? What new principle/term/concept was learned through this assignment? Do I understand democratic principles completely?

Suggestions on how this can be accomplished:

- Students isolate important information and write them down.
- Students list democratic principles and individual perceptions about each.
- Students need to predetermined when they will write information (before, during, after class, for homework).
- Students need to predetermine amount of time they are going to devote to journaling task (five minutes each day, period, etc.).
- Reflection process:
- Think about future potential uses,
- Applications,
- Practice or application in settings other than classroom.

FIGURE 6.6 STATEMENT JOURNAL

EXAMPLE STANDARDS

Language Arts-Writing 4th Grade

1.2d Conclude with a paragraph that summarizes the points.

History-Social Science- Historical and Social Sciences Analysis Skills K-5th Grades

1 Students summarize key events and explain those events…

- **Active Learning Implications:** Students learn to write a short statement, phrase, or word to summarize a theory, concept, topic, or subject matter.

- **Goal:** From the above two example standards, students need to:

    1. Write summary paragraphs.

    2. Summarize and explain details of key events.

- **Active Learners Responsibility:** To be responsible and invest effort to improve listening, reading, and memorization skills. To explain in detail, with as few words as possible, a theory, concept, topic, etc.

- **Student Responsive Design in Practice**

    Academics: Students need to know the standards the assignment is based on. This helps establish purpose and reason for academic mastery. Students also need to understand the assessment criteria and the due date. This will help focus their efforts to complete the task correctly and in a timely manner.

    Social/Collaborative: Students can develop study groups to receive constructive feedback on their summary skills and paragraphs. A game can be developed amongst the participants to see who could use the fewest words to summarize a given topic.

    Contextual: Students need to tie assignment into the specific context of the time, lesson, etc. to reinforce their learning.

    Cognitive/Developmental: Students need to ask themselves; do I need more background information, key vocabulary, or use a different strategy to learn material effectively? How well do I listen? How can I stay more focused? What is distracting me? Have I listed key events? Why do I think that these events are key?

Suggestions on how this can be accomplished:

- Students isolate information to be learned (this can be by class, period, subject, etc.).

- Students establish key events checklist.

- Students establish how many details a key event needs to have.

- Reflection process:

- What is the task at hand?

- What basic information needs to be known?

- Decide how material read can be reduced to a simple concept or word.

- Write a paragraph on how chosen word or phrase was determined. Express in writing precisely what word or single phrase was intended to do.

FIGURE 6.7 CLASS ASSIGNMENT JOURNALS

EXAMPLE STANDARDS

Visual and Performing Arts 3rd Grade

5.3 Explain how the time management, problem solving, and self-disciplining skills …apply to other school activities.

English Language Development 6th-12th Grades

Use strategies of note taking, outlining, and summarizing…

- **Active Learning Implications:** Students learn how to keep accurate and up to date timelines concerning class assignments. They also record insight about learning and strategy use.

- **Goal:** From the above two example standards, students need to:

  1. Demonstrate how time management, problem solving, and other self disciplining strategies apply to other activities.

  2. Demonstrate the use of note taking, outlining, and summarizing skills regularly.

Active Learners Responsibility: To be responsible for keeping a record of assignments due, self-improvement and how to attain higher academic achievement. Students need to continually monitor and improve their organizational skills, time management and problem-solving strategies.

- **Student Responsive Design in Practice**

  Academics: Students need to know the standards the assignment is based on. This helps establish purpose and reason for academic mastery. Students also need to understand the assessment criteria and the due date. This will help focus their efforts to complete the task correctly and in a timely manner.

  Social/Collaborative: Students can talk to each other to motivate and keep each other on track. Students write suggestions in journals on how to use time more efficiently.

  Contextual: Students need to be able to complete assignments within realistic time constraints. By keeping a journal, students will be able to track progress and keep assignment requirements fresh in their minds.

  Cognitive/Developmental: Students need to ask themselves; do I need more background information, key vocabulary, or use a different strategy to learn material effectively? Am I going to complete task within time frame? What do I need to rear-range in my schedule? Do I honestly understand all the requirements to complete the task successfully? Am I using note taking skills to learn more efficiently or am I just trying to get through an assignment?

Suggestions on how this can be accomplished:

- Students need to learn to write down class assignments in notebook, agenda, etc.

- Students need to develop the ability to jot down and document how they went about doing task, e.g., steps taken, process, etc.

- Reflection process:

- What/did any errors or mistakes occur?

- Was their any area of difficulty or misunderstanding?

- What about this assignment was the easiest for you?

- Are there any strategies that I need to quit using?

- List one new strategy that can be used to get work done more efficiently.

FIGURE 6.8 RESTATE/REPHRASE STRATEGIES

EXAMPLE STANDARDS

English Language Development-Listening and Speaking 6th-12th Grades

Restate in simple terms the main ides of presentations and subject matter content.

Mathematics-Statistics, Data Analysis, and Probability 4th Grade

1.0 Students organize, represent, and interpret numerical and categorical data and clearly communicate their findings.

- **Active Learning Implications:** Students learn to put concepts into terms that make sense to them. This gives them the skill to effectively communicate information to others because they fully understand material themselves.

- **Goal:** From the above two example standards, students need to:

  1. Restate main ideas in student terms.

  2. Organize, represent, and interpret data clearly to others.

- **Active Learners Responsibility:** To be responsible to learn and internalize ab-stract information theories, concepts, and subject matter in words and terms that makes sense to the students, and can be adequately explained to others..

- **Student Responsive Design in Practice**

Academics: Students need to know the standards the assignment is based on. This helps establish purpose and reason for academic mastery. Students also need to understand the assessment criteria and the due date. This will help focus their efforts to complete the task correctly and in a timely manner.

Social/Collaborative: Students can develop the ability to articulate clearly to others. They can practice in front of others and receive constructive feedback. In this process they will also be able to understand the information being learned on a much deeper level.

Contextual: By being able to restate and rephrase, students will be able to understand information in context as well as applying that information to other settings to accomplish a task. Data without context means little, organizing it will help students understand abstract mathematical terminology.

Cognitive/Developmental: Students need to ask themselves; do I need more background information, key vocabulary, or use a different strategy to learn material effectively? To rephrase, requires a deeper level of understanding, are there other concepts that I need to understand more fully to present this information to others?

Suggestions on how this can be accomplished:

- Students need to learn how to isolate important information, concept, theory, etc.
- Material can be written in a journal, note card, or in an electronic format.
- Students can practice various mathematical models inputting data and graphing results.
- Reflection process:
- Think about potential uses,
- Applications,
- How to restate information adequately to others.
- Students get the bigger picture of the "why"

FIGURE 6.9 STRATEGY STEPS

EXAMPLE STANDARDS

Science-Investigation and Experimentation 2nd Grade

4d Write or draw out descriptions of a sequence of steps, events, observations.

English Language Development

After an activity, present a brief report demonstrating 3 or 4 simple steps necessary to achieve a specific goal or product…

- **Active Learning Implications:** Students list specific steps on how they solved a problem, dilemma, or resolve a conflict. They understand and can communicate the process in detail.

- **Goal:** From the above two example standards, students need to:
  1. Write out descriptions of observations, steps, or events.
  2. Write brief report limiting description to three or four steps.

- **Active Learners Responsibility:** To be responsible for processing information into a tangible set of steps and be able to communicate and perform steps to others in a logical and sequential fashion.

- **Student Responsive Design in Practice**

  Academics: Students need to know the standards the assignment is based on. This helps establish purpose and reason for academic mastery. Students also need to understand the assessment criteria and the due date. This will help focus their efforts to complete the task correctly and in a timely manner.

  Social/Collaborative: Students can develop study groups to describe the steps they came up with to complete their assignment. They can also collaborate to come up with better more precise steps on what they did or attempted to do.

  Contextual: Whenever steps in sequence are described, context must be understood in detail. This assignment is a great opportunity for students to hone these types of skills.

  Cognitive/Developmental: To develop this skill adequately, students have to know and understand what they are doing in great detail. This process will help the student identify any gaps they have in their thinking.

Suggestions on how this can be accomplished:

- Create an observation checklist.
- Create a format that can only list four steps.
- Have students focus on process and not on the end result.
- Process to be understood, must be broken down into several small segments.
- Steps need to be listed in the order they occurred.
- Reflection process (Can approach be adapted or modified?)

- Was strategy productive?
- Was it time efficient?

FIGURE 6.10 DEVELOPING ANALYTICAL SKILLS

EXAMPLE STANDARDS

Language Arts-Listening and Speaking 8th Grade

1.9 Interpret and evaluate the various ways in which visual image maker (e.g., graphic artist, illustrators, news photographers) communicate information and affect impressions and opinions.

History-Social Science-Historical and Social Sciences Analysis Skills K-5th Grades

5 Students judge the significance…and analyze how relative advantages or disadvantages can change over time.

- **Active Learning Implications:** Students analyze advantages or disadvantages of choices that they make on a specific topic.

- **Goal:** From the above two example standards, students need to:

  1. Interpret and evaluate visuals and the message conveyed by the originator.

  2. Judge significance of an event and the advantages/disadvantages over time.

- **Active Learners Responsibility:** To respond appropriately, develop objectivity, and listen to others when personal opinions may differ.

- **Student Responsive Design in Practice**

  Academics: Students need to know the standards the assignment is based on. This helps establish purpose and reason for academic mastery. Students also need to understand the assessment criteria and the due date. This will help focus their efforts to complete the task correctly and in a timely manner.

  Social/Collaborative: Students can develop the ability to articulate what they are seeing or interpreting to others. Ground rules need to be established so that students can express their interpretations.

  Contextual: Evaluation and interpretation can be done in a free-form format or within very specific contextual restraints. Students need to be able to adjust their strategies to conform to the assignments requirements.

  Cognitive/Developmental: Students need to understand how to view an artifact and explain or analyze it to others.

Suggestions on how this can be accomplished:

- Create checklist to analyze posters/cartoon/etc. with possible examples.

- Create advantage/disadvantage worksheet as a helping device.

- Students isolate on a specific issue of concern.

- Students list several alternatives to their initial opinions.

- Students provide a rationale for choice selections.

- Reflection process.

- Can be written in a journal, essay, notes, or electronic media.

FIGURE 6.11 TIME ON TASK STRATEGIES

EXAMPLE STANDARDS

Language Arts-Writing 11th Grade

1.7 Use systematic strategies to organize and record information.

Mathematics-Probability and Statistics 8th-12th Grades

8.0 Students organize and describe distribution of data by using a number of different methods, including frequency, tables, histograms, standard line and bar graphs, stem-and-leaf displays, scatter plots, and box-and-whisker plots.

Visual and Performing Arts-Theater 9th-12th Grades

5.2 Manage time, prioritize responsibilities, and meet completion deadlines…

- **Active Learning Implications:** Students record how much time is available to study versus how much time that they actually spend studying.

- **Goal:** From the above three example standards, students need to:

  1. Systematic strategy used to organize and record information.

  2. Organize and describe different graphing mechanisms for differing purposes.

  3. Manage time, prioritize timelines to meet deadlines.

- **Active Learners Responsibility:** To be responsible and focused, understanding the concept of time management. Continually evaluate and learn more effective ways to utilize and organize timelines..

- **Student Responsive Design in Practice**

  Academics: Students need to know the standards the assignment is based on. This helps establish purpose and reason for academic mastery. Students also need to understand the assessment criteria and the due date. This will help focus their efforts to complete the task correctly and in a timely manner.

Social/Collaborative: Students can develop a check and balance system with a partner to make sure they are staying on task. They can also receive feedback on better or more effective time management task,

Contextual: Students can graph material in a way that they can monitor their progress. This skill can be transferred to many other areas and disciplines.

Cognitive/Developmental: Students need to understand how to read graphs, do plotting, and manage their time.

Suggestions on how this can be accomplished:

- Create activities deadline sheet. Are timelines being met?

- Use several different methods to demonstrate using the same math problem or solution.

- Students draw a time frame of the hours in one day

- Students log in what they do in increments of some specific time frame, e.g., 30 minutes, 60 minutes, etc.

- Reflection process:

- Where is time wasted the most?

- When is time used most effectively?

- What changes can be implemented?

FIGURE 6.12 ACTIVE LISTENING SKILLS

EXAMPLE STANDARDS

Language Arts-Listening and Speaking 1st Grade

1.0 Students listen critically and respond appropriately…

Language Arts-Listening and Speaking 11th Grade

1.0 Student formulates adroit arguments…and delivers focused and coherent presentations that convey clear and distinct perspectives and solid reasoning.

- **Active Learning Implication:** Students practice active listening to stay focused and to mentally challenge themselves to stay on task.

- **Goal:** From the above two example standards, students need to:

  1. Listen critically and respond appropriately.

  2. Deliver focused arguments that are clear, coherent, and logical.

- **Active Learners Responsibility:** To be responsible for self-monitoring behavior. Students need to monitor concentration levels and learn to actively listen to teaching as it is occurring. Students need to identify distractions in the classroom and set up strategies to overcome these barriers to concentration and learning.

- **Student Responsive Design in Practice**

Academics: Students need to know the standards the assignment is based on. This helps establish purpose and reason for academic mastery. Students also need to understand the assessment criteria and the due date. This will help focus their efforts to complete the task correctly and in a timely manner.

Social/Collaborative: Students can practice responding appropriately in front of others. It is also an excellent practice to learn to both give and receive constructive feedback.

Contextual: Students learn to listen and respond in specific settings for specific purposes.

Cognitive/Developmental: Students need to develop mature and appropriate responses to others and their arguments.

Suggestions on how this can be accomplished:

- Create checklist to focus speeches in a coherent and clear fashion.

- Students need to set a specific time frame to monitor their listening time on task e.g., 5, 10, 20 minutes, etc.

- At these intervals, students need to do a quick mental or paper and pencil check in.

- Reflection process:

- What is being taught at that exact minute?

- Is information being understood?

- Are notes being taken?

- Are you letting you thoughts drift to other distractions.

- Repeat at each predetermined time interval.

FIGURE 6.13 RECALL, SUMMARIZE, CONCERNS, CONNECTIONS, AND COMMENTS (RS3Q STRATEGY)

EXAMPLE STANDARDS

Language Arts-Listening and Speaking 6th Grade

2.5 Theorize on the causes and effect of problems and establishes connections between the defined problem and solution. Offers evidence to validate proposed solutions.

Language Arts-Writing 9th-10th Grades

1.5 Synthesize information from multiple sources and identify complexities and discrepancies in the information and the different perspectives found in each...

- **Active Learning Implications:** Students develop skills to enhance their ability to recall, summarize, ask questions, address concerns and comments and how this all relates back to them and their connections to various applications.

- **Goal:** From the above two example standards, students need to:

  1. Theorize cause and effect situations with plausible solutions.

  2. Synthesize information from multiple sources.

- **Active Learners responsibility:** To be responsible to self-monitor and actively engage in cognitive activities that synthesize and integrate information. This in turn enhances study skills.

- **Student Responsive Design in Practice**

  Academics: Students need to know the standards the assignment is based on. This helps establish purpose and reason for academic mastery. Students also need to understand the assessment criteria and the due date. This will help focus their efforts to complete the task correctly and in a timely manner.

  Social/Collaborative: Students can develop study groups to go over how they analyze a theory or concept. They can also discuss several causes and effects and the solutions to each problem

  Contextual: Students can evaluate cause and effect in specific settings and also expand the theory to alternative scenarios.

  Cognitive/Developmental: Students need to ask themselves; do I need more background information about cause and effect? Do I understand the background information significantly?

Suggestions on how this can be accomplished:

- Create a cause and effect matrix to list responses.

- Use a cross reference checklist to organize and synthesize materials.

- Students need to develop an individual approach to enhance recall e.g., word list, phrase, index card notes, agenda, etc.

- Students summarize recall process into specific but brief points or bullets.

- Students' writes down any concerns they have about understanding, application, etc.

- Students list possible applications, generalizations, or links to other materials, etc.

- Reflection process:

- Students write down any self-awareness comments on what they learned during this topic, task, or assignment.

To sum up the essence and purpose of listing these twelve active learning strategies:

The more students can take responsibility for their own learning, the more likely they are to attribute success to their own efforts. If students believe that their efforts will make a difference in what and how much they learn, then they are more likely to expend higher levels of effort in their studies (Hagen and Weinstein, 1995, p. 53).

Understanding students' strategy use and its direct relationship to their academic success is important for both the teacher and student. Students take personal ownership over their learning and thinking strategies, which over time produces self-confidence and self-efficacy.

CHARACTERISTICS OF ACTIVE LEARNING

Research shows that students who are active learners, approach their academic task with confidence, and tend to work more diligently, no matter how difficult the assignments may be. The more assignments completed, the more confident students become, and the more automatic their strategy selection evolves (Bargh and Chartrand, 1999; James, 1958).

Active learning by students can be considered successful when students can describe in detail their own learning process. This is what the twelve examples from above were meant to demonstrate. The students become competent in how they plan, monitor, use rubrics, and other assessment devices to evaluate their learning. They possess a level of control over their learning in that they understand how to apply strategies to increase their academic proficiency. They also have a repertoire of differing strategies at their disposal which help them;

- Understand academic information and explanations presented orally;

- Can explain relevance of academic standards taught and how it applies to them;

- Can explain purpose of performance assessments and how they will master that purpose;

- Can discuss and answer questions on academic topics discussed in class;

- Knows how to question teacher for clarification on directions;

- Can engage in academic communication with both the teacher and peers;
- Understands and applies strategies to learning content specific and academic vocabulary;
- Can utilize schema building with graphing, mapping, and charting;
- Can articulate in detail how an answer was formulated or derived;
- Can present various styles of oral reports depending on purpose and audience;
- Can read for different purposes in content textbooks, authentic texts, library and trade books, as well as different reference materials;
- Can write short and long answers to questions about content studied;
- Can write content-specific text (e.g., narrative, expository, lab notes, problem solutions);
- Can explain their ability to complete classroom task in detail; and finally,
- Active learners can describe and explain in detail their own plan of progress in terms of monitoring and evaluating their learning activities.

These students believe and attribute their academic performance to their own efforts (including learning strategies) rather than to circumstances outside of their control?

SUMMARY

Classrooms that utilize active teaching and learning strategies promote an environment that engages all students in relevant activities that empower as well as support their learning. The teachers in these classrooms have established a climate that minimizes anxiety, promotes fairness and self-efficacy, which in turn motivates student participation and respects the diversity of all. These instructional practices support academic, contextual, developmental, and social responsibilities, which involve students in collaborative work to master important content, concepts, and skills. Data dissemination, which is a foundation of the methodology espoused in this book, promotes the planning and implementation of quality classroom procedures, routines, and an approach to learning in a variety of configurations and techniques that support meaningful student learning. Lastly, when teachers embrace these philosophical constructs:

- They use their instructional time effectively to incorporate the students various learning modalities.

- They address the students' academic, social, cognitive and developmental levels.

- They promote high academic standards for all students.

- They strive for mastery in all content and subject matter areas.

In addition, these teachers reinforce self-efficacy by encouraging students to show their work often. This dynamic gives teachers an opportunity to provide feedback, praise, guidance, and reinforce positive habits that benefits the students, and it makes them active collaborators in their learning. Students actively learn to take the initiative, monitor their growth, set realistic timelines, and in turn, teachers hold them accountable. This accountability translates into students who have taken ownership concerning their learning. For all students to reach their potential, they need to understand that academic success is a process of degrees based on their efforts. Thus, academic productivity is influenced by the students' desire and effort in and out of the classroom, along with their personal commitment for success.

FINAL REFLECTION

In summary, all components of active teaching and learning are interwoven with each influencing the other. The cognitive/developmental portions are evidenced throughout the other components. It makes no sense to teach an academic standard when a student does not understand the words or concepts being taught. The social/collaborative portion is a waste of valuable instructional time if it is not at the appropriate cognitive and academic levels. Contextualization bonds to nothing without a context or reference point that anchors the lesson. And finally, none of these instructional practices makes sense unless the students are valued, their circumstances analyzed, and specific academic interventions are defined, to promote each student's success.

Making meaningful teaching and learning for students a reality requires a reexamination of core values, and to revisit the reason education as a profession was chosen in the first place. Those of us who work daily with students understand the influence we have on students' lives, as well as the important roles that we play.

If we allow ourselves to overlook the learning potential in any of our children, if we focus on their school problems…we may succumb to the medical model, wherein any deviation in a child's academic path is viewed as if it were some sort of disease or dysfunction that must be treated with a dose of this or that…he or she is not wrong or bad or dumb for seeking other ways to learn, but rather has not yet adjusted to the school's way of learning (Fried, 2001, pp. 128-129).

As outstanding teachers and administrators, it is of paramount importance that we collectively encourage student empowerment. We, as educators, need to understand and value our students. We know that students need to feel that someone cares, that the students have some control over their learning—therefore their destiny, and that the students have competencies to do their work successfully.

One hundred percent of our students doing well, clearly that's the right goal. Many ...argue that it is not attainable...I believe that when it comes to learning, we can replace the bell curve with the 'J' curve. Consider the 'J'—it starts at the bottom and ends at the top...How do we do a really good job with 100 percent of our students?...Sixty–five percent [of all students] deserve the answer Mahthey, 2004, p. 23).

In other words, the solution for the sixty-five percent is found in us and our profession. As educational leaders, we need to continually do our homework. We accomplish this by analyzing our data, using formative, summative, process, and demographic information, to understand our students' needs. We are successfully identifying barriers to learning, and use different instructional strategies to overcome them. This approach results in a positive environment that is standards based and optimizes student success. We understand our students' needs, and give them guidance and encouragement. In a sense, we have the same hope for them as we would have for our own children.

In reality, for all students, it is the educator's caring, foresightedness, experience, and wisdom, which will ultimately guide and direct them. By students giving us their time and effort today, we can give back to them the tools and skills that they will need to succeed tomorrow. Active teaching and learning strategies will help us achieve the goal of NCLB by 2013. That is, 100 percent of our students succeeding at the proficient and advanced levels. Not only will the students obtain their academic goals, but will mature emotionally, developmentally, and cognitively as well. This blueprint is essential in facilitating the students' quest for self-efficacy, empowerment, and ultimately becoming self-sustaining and life-long learners.

REFERENCES

Ames, C. (1992). Classrooms: Goals, structures, and student motivation. *Journal of Educational Psychology, 84,* pp. 261-271.

Anderson, L. (2002). Curricular alignment: A re-examination. *Theory into Practice (41)* 4 pp. 255-260.

Anderson, L. (Ed.), Krathwohl, D. (Ed.), Airasian, P., Cruikshank, K., Mayer, R. Pintrich, P., Raths, J. and Wittrock, M. (2001). A taxonomy for learning, teaching and assessing: A revision of Bloom's Taxonomy of Educational Objectives. New York: Longman.

Anderman, E., Griesinger, T., and Westerfield, G, (1998). Motivation and cheating during early adolescence. *Journal of Educational Psychology, 90,* 84-93.

Ashton, P., and Webb, R. (1986). *Making a difference: Teachers' sense of efficacy and student achievement.* New York: Longman.

Bandura, A. (1993). Perceived self-effacacy in cognitive development and functioning. *Educational Psychologist, 28,* pp. 117-148.

Bandura, A. (1997). *Self-efficacy: The exercise of control.* New York: W.H. Freeman.

Bargh, J., and Chartrand, T. (1999). The unbearable automaticity of being. *American Psychologist, 4,* pp. 462-479.

Beck, I., Mckeown, J., Hamilton, R., and Kucan, L. (1997). *Questioning the author: An approach for enhancing student engagement with text.* Newark, DE: International Reading Association.

Bernhardt, V. (2003). No schools left behind. *Educational Leadership.* February, 2003, 26-30.

Bonney, M. (1969). Self-becoming as self-growth. *Theory into Practice.* VII, (3) pp. 143-148.

Borich, G., and Tombaci, M. (1997). *Educational psychology: A contemporary approach.* 2nd Edition. NY: Addison-Wesley Educational Publishers Inc.

Borkowski, J. (1992). Metacognitive theory: A framework for teaching literacy, writing,and math skills. *Journal of Learning Disabilities, 25,* pp. 253-257.

Rock and Michelle Moore MiRoc Publishing @ AOL.Com

Branford, J., Brown, A., and Cocking, R. (Eds.) (1999). *How people learn: Brain, mind, experience, and school*. Washington, DC: National Academy Press.

Butler, D. and Winne, P. (1995). Feedback and self-regulated learning: A theoretical synthesis. *Review of educational research, 65* pp. 245-281.

California State Board of Education. (1997). *English-Language Arts Content Standards for California Public Schools Kindergarten through Grade Twelve*. Department of Education, Sacramento, CA

California State Board of Education. (1998). *History-Social Science Content Standards for California Public Schools Kindergarten through Grade Twelve*. Department of Education, Sacramento, CA

California State Board of Education. (1997). *Mathematics Content Standards for California Public Schools Kindergarten through Grade Twelve*. Department of Education, Sacramento, CA

California State Board of Education. (1998). *English-Language Arts Content Standards for California Public Schools Kindergarten through Grade Twelve*. Department of Education, Sacramento, CA

California State Board of Education. (2001). *Visual and Performing Arts Content Standards California Public Schools Kindergarten through Grade Twelve*. Department of Education, Sacramento, CA

California State Board of Education. (1997). *English Language Development for California Public Schools Kindergarten through Grade Twelve*. Department of Education, Sacramento, CA

Carroll, J. (1963). A model of schooling. *Teachers College Record, 64*, pp. 723-733.

Combs, A.W. (1982). Affect education or none at all. *Educational Leadership*. April, 1982, 495-497.

Cooley, C. (1902). *Human nature and the social order*. New York: Scriber.

Cotton, K. (2000). *The schooling practices that matter most*. Association of Supervisor and Curriculum Developers. Alexandria, VA

Daniels, D., and Kalman, D. (2001). Revealing children's perceptions of classroom practices: Using multiple approaches. In *Integrating what we know about learners and learning: A foundation for transferring PreK-20 practices*. Symposium at the annual meeting of the American Educational Association, Seattle, WA

Dewey, J. (1916). *Democracy in education*. New York: The Macmillian Co.

Dorn, L., and Soffos, C. (2001). *Shaping literate minds: Developing self-regulated learners*. Portland, MA: Stenhouse.

Education Trust, The. (2000). *Achievement in America 2000*. Washington, DC Susan Jones Sears.

Edwards, D., and Mercer, N. (1987). *Common knowledge: The development of understanding in the classroom*. London, UK: Routledge.

Elder, L., and Paul, R. (2001). *How to study and learn: A discipline using critical thinking concepts and tools*. Foundation for Critical Thinking. Dillion Beach: CA

Fried, R. (2001). Passionate learners and the challenge of schooling. *Phi Delta Kappan* Vol. 83 (2). pp. 124-136.

Glickman, C. (2001). Dichotzing Education: Why no one wins and America Loses. *Phi Delta Kappan* October, pp. 147-152.

Good, T., and Brophy, J. (2002). *Looking in classrooms*. 8th Edition. New York: Longman.

Graham, S., Harris, K. and Reid, R. (1992). Developing self-regulated learners. *Focus on Exceptional Children, 24,* pp. 1-16.

Grahman, S., and Golan, S. (1991). Motivational influences on cognition: Task involvement, ego involvement, and depth of information processing. *Journal of Educational Psychology, 83,* 187-196.

Gusky, T. (1980). Master learning: Applying the theory. *Theory into Practice (19)* 2 pp.104-111.

Hagen, A. and Weinstein, C. (1995). Achievement goals, self-regulated learning, and the role of classroom context. *New Directions for Teaching and Learning, 63,* pp. 43-55.

Halliday, M. (1985). *Three aspects of children's language development: Learn language, learn about language, learn through language*. Unpublished manuscript, Department of Linguistics, University of Sydney, Austrailia.

Holdaway, D. (1979). *The foundations of literacy*. Sydney: Aston Scholastic.

Hogan. D. M., and Tudge, J.R.H., (1999). Implications of Vygotsky's theory for peer Learning. In A.M. O'Donnel and A. King (Eds.), *Cognitive perspectives on peer learning* (pp. 39-65). Mahwah, NJ: Erlbaum.

Jamentz, Kate. (2001). Beyond data mania. *Leadership*. Nov./Dec. 2001, 8-11.

James, W. (1958). *Talks to teachers*. New York: Norton.

Kiewra, K. (2000). How teachers can help students learn and teach them how to learn. *Theory into Practice, Vol. 41* (2) pp. 71-80.

Lester, F. (1994). Musing about mathematical problem-solving research: 1970-1994. *Journal for Research in Mathematics Education, 25,* pp. 660-675.

Lewis, Anne. (2003). A Continuing American Dream. *Phi Delta Kappan*. Vol. 85 (4) pp. 259-260.

MacKinnon, D. (1978). *In search of human effectiveness: Identifying and developing creativity*. Buffalo, NY: Creative Education Foundation.

Martinez-Pons, M. (1996). Test of a model of parental excitement of academic self regulation. *Journal of Experimental Education, 64*, pp. 213-227.

McCarney, S., Wunderlich, K., Bauer, A. (1993). *Pre-Referral Intervention Manuel* Columbia, MO: Hawthorne Educational Services, Inc.

Manthey, George. (2004). 'Sorta dumb' beliefs fail 65% of Students. *Leadership.* Vol 33 (5) p. 23.

McCombs, B. (2003). A framework for the redesign of K-12 education in the context of current educational reform. *Theory into Practice,* (42) 2.

McCombs, B. and Whisler, S. (1997). *The Learner-centered classroom and school.* San Francisco, CA: Jossey Bass.

Meece, J. (2003). Applying learner-centered principles to middle school education. *Theory into Practice,* Spring 2003, (42) 2.

Mitra, D. (2002). Making it real: Involving youth in school reform. In *Student Voices and Democracy in Schools.* International Symposium of the American Educational Research Association, New Orleans, LA.

Moore, R. (1999a). Academic Standards and School Accountability. *The National Forum of Educational Administration and Supervision Journal* Vol 16E (4).

Moore, R. (1999b). School Leadership that Promotes a Dynamic School Culture. *The National Forum of Teacher Education Journal Vol. 9E (3).*

Moore, R. and Moore, M. A. (2004). Using a data driven balanced Pedagogy: No Child Left Behind. (in press).

Nelson-Le Gall, and Resnick, L. (1998). Help seeking, achievement motivation, and the social practice of intelligence in school. In S.A. Karabenick (Ed.), *Strategic help seeking: Implications for learning and teaching* (pp. 39-60). Hillsdale, NJ: Erlbaum.

O'Shea, M. (2003). Teaching to the standards. *Leadership Vol. 31* (3) pp. 22-23).

Perkins, D.N. (1985). *Where Is Creativity?* Paper presented at the University of Iowa Second Annual Humanities Symposium, Iowa City, CA

Pajares, F. (2002). Gender and perceived self-effacacy. *Theory into Practice.* Vol. 41 (2) pp. 116-125.

Pelligrini, A. and Blatchford, P. (2000). *The child at school: Interactions with peers and teachers.* New York: Oxford Press.

Pianta, R. (1995). *Enhancing relationships between children and teachers.* Washington DC: American Psychological Association.

Piaget, L. (1973). *To understand is to invent. The future of education.* New York: Viking Press.

Piaget, J. (1976). *The psychology of intelligence.* New York: Viking Press.

Piaget, L. (1981). *Intelligence and affectivity. Their relationship during child Development*. Palo Alto, CA: Annual Reviews, Inc.

Pressley, M., and Afflerbach, P. (1995). *Verbal protocols of reading: The nature of constructively responsive reading*. Hilsdale, NJ: Erlbaum.

Pressley, M., and Wharton-McDonald, R. (1997). Skilled comprehension and its development through instruction. *School Psychology Review, 26,* pp. 448-466.

Raths, J. (2002). Improving instruction. *Theory into Practice*. Vol. 41 (4) pp.233-237.

Ryan, R., and Stiller, J. (1991). The social contexts of internalization: Parent and teacher influences on autonomy, motivation, and learning. In P. Pintrich and M. Maehr (Eds.), *Advances in motivation and achievement, Vol. 7, Goals and self-regulatory processes* (pp. 115-149). Greenwich, CT: JAI Press.

Sears, S. and House, R. (2002). Preparing school counselors to be leaders and advocates: A critical need in the new millennium. *Theory in Practice,* Vol. 41 (3) pp. 154-162.

Schunk, D. (1983). Developing children's self-efficacy and skills: Te role of social comparative information and goal setting. *Contemporary Educational Psychology 8,* pp. 76-86.

Schunk, D. (1987). Peer models and children's behavioral change. *Review of Educational Research, 57,* pp. 149-174.

Schmoker, M. (1999). *Results: The key to continuous school improvement.* 2[Nd] Edition Alexander, VA: Association of Supervisors and Curriculum Developers.

Shannon, S. (2003). *Nine characteristics of high-performing schools: A research based resource for school leadership teams to assist with the school improvement process.* Office of Superintendent of Public Instruction, Olympia, WA

Stipek, D., (2002). Good instruction is motivating. In A. Wigfield and J.S. Eccles (Eds.) *Development of achievement motivation* (pp. 310-334). New York: Academic Press.

Sullivan, M. (1997). A meta-analysis of experimental research studies based on the Dunn and Dunn learning style model and its relationship to academic achievement and performance. *National Forum of Applied Educational Research Journal* . Vol. 10 (1) pp. 3-11.

Sturtevant, E. (1998). What middle and high school educators need to know about language minority students. *NASSP Bulletin, 82*(600), pp. 73-77.

Thompson, S. (2003). Creating a high-performance school system. *Phi Delta Kappan.* Vol. 84 (7), pp. 489-495.

Urdan, T., Midgley, C., and Anderman, E. (1998). The role of classroom goal structure in students' use of self-handicapping strategies. *American Educational Research Journal, 35,* 101-135.

Valeski, T., and Stipek, D. (2001). Young children's feelings about school. *Child Developmen, 72* (4), pp. 1198-1213.

Woolfolk Hoy, A. and Tschannen-Moran, A. (1999). Implications of cognitive approaches to peer learning for teacher education. In A.M. O,Donnel and A. King (Eds.), *Cognitive perspectives on peer learning.* (pp. 257-284). Mahwah, NJ: Erlbaum.

Webb, N.M., Troper, J.D., and Fall, R. (1995). Constructive activity and learning in collaborative small groups. *Journal of Educational Psychology, 87,* 406-423. Weinberger, E. and McCombs, B. (2003). Appling the LCPs to high school education.*Theory into Practice,* Spring 2003, (42) 2.

Zimmerman, B.J. (1989). A social cognitive view of self-regulated academic learning. *Journal of Educational Psychology, 81,* 329-339.

Zimmermann, B., Bonner, S., and Kovach, R. (1996). *Developing self-regulated learners: Beyond achievement to self-effacacy.* Washington, DC: American Psychology Association.

THE AUTHORS

Rock D Moore Ed.D is an Administrator in the Adelanto Elementary School District and a professor at Chapman University. He received his Doctorate from The University of Sarasota, Florida in 1996. He has written over fifty articles on various issues surrounding education and has done educational consultations for the last seven years at the Local, National, and International levels.

Michelle A. Moore M.Ed. is an Administrator in the Orange Unified School District. She has a Masters Degree in Cross-cultural Education with a Specialization in Curriculum and Instruction. She was recently accepted into the University of Southern California's Doctoral Program in Urban Education. She has spoken at the National and International levels on issues surrounding data driven instruction.

ISBN 141203660-7